Paulo Freire

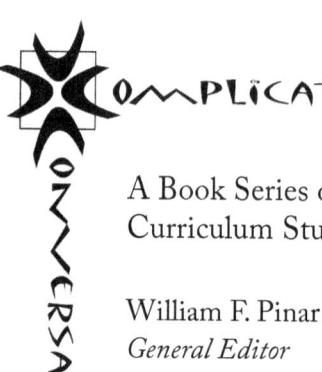

Complicated Conversation

A Book Series of
Curriculum Studies

William F. Pinar
General Editor

Volume 54

The Complicated Conversation series is part of the Peter Lang Education list.
Every volume is peer reviewed and meets
the highest quality standards for content and production.

PETER LANG
New York • Bern • Berlin
Brussels • Vienna • Oxford • Warsaw

Peter Roberts

Paulo Freire

Philosophy, Pedagogy, and Practice

PETER LANG
New York • Bern • Berlin
Brussels • Vienna • Oxford • Warsaw

Library of Congress Cataloging-in-Publication Control Number: 2022005997

Bibliographic information published by **Die Deutsche Nationalbibliothek**.
Die Deutsche Nationalbibliothek lists this publication in the "Deutsche
Nationalbibliografie"; detailed bibliographic data are available
on the Internet at http://dnb.d-nb.de/.

ISSN 1534-2816
ISBN 978-1-4331-9518-1 (hardcover)
ISBN 978-1-4331-9519-8 (paperback)
ISBN 978-1-4331-6126-1 (ebook pdf)
ISBN 978-1-4331-6127-8 (epub)
DOI 10.3726/b19437

© 2022 Peter Lang Publishing, Inc., New York
80 Broad Street, 5th floor, New York, NY 10004
www.peterlang.com

All rights reserved.
Reprint or reproduction, even partially, in all forms such as microfilm,
xerography, microfiche, microcard, and offset strictly prohibited.

Table of Contents

Introduction: Paulo Freire: Continuing the Conversation   vii

Chapter One: Philosophy, Pedagogy, and Practice: The Work of Paulo Freire   1

Chapter Two: Learning to Live with Doubt: Kierkegaard, Freire, and Critical Pedagogy   25

Chapter Three: Impure Neoliberalism: A Freirean Critique of Dominant Trends in Higher Education   41

Chapter Four: Thesis Supervision: A Freirean Approach   57

Chapter Five: Knowledge, Culture, and Education: Freire and Dilemmas of Difference   71

Chapter Six: Education, Ethics, and Leadership: Camus, Freire, and Covid-19   89

Chapter Seven: Conscientization, Compassion, and Madness: Freire, Barreto, and the Limits of Education   101

References   121

Credits   137

Introduction

Paulo Freire: Continuing the Conversation

When an important intellectual figure dies, there is often a period of renewed interest in his or her work. Obituaries are written and legacies are assessed. Sometimes special issues of journals will be organized to acknowledge the contribution that has been made. In most cases, this additional attention begins to abate after a few months or years. Paulo Freire has defied this logic. Freire passed away in May 1997, and while there were certainly many tributes paid to him in the concluding years of the 20th century, there has, against the usual trend, been no diminution of interest in the two decades that have followed in the 21st century. Freire's ideas have continued to be discussed, debated, and applied by theorists and practitioners in a multiplicity of different fields. Numerous books, articles, chapters, and theses have been devoted to Freirean themes over the last twenty years. The posthumous publication of work by Freire that had hitherto been unpublished or enjoyed only limited circulation has certainly played a part in generating new interest. Books such as *Pedagogy of Indignation* (Freire, 2004) and *Daring to Dream* (Freire, 2007) are particularly notable in this respect. Some of the material published, or currently being prepared, has also been driven by key dates such as the 50th anniversary of Freire's landmark text, *Pedagogy of the Oppressed*, and the centenary of his birth. But these initiatives have only added to what was already a steady stream of new scholarly work. The perspectives adopted by those who have contributed to this scholarly conversation have varied widely, but regardless of the positions taken by the many commentators, it has been clear that Freire's ideas are worthy of continuing reflection and engagement.

How has the world changed since May 1997? It is difficult to know where to begin in answering this question, but some pivotal moments and developments that readily spring to mind include the World Trade Center attacks in September 2001, the wars in Afghanistan and Iraq, the rise of China as a dominant world power, the global financial crisis, a growing awareness of the alarming consequences of climate change, the emergence of new forms of political populism with the election of leaders such as President Trump (in the United States) and President Bolsanaro (in Brazil), the 'Me Too' and 'Black Lives Matter' movements, the powerful role now being played by tech giants and social media in shaping patterns of thought and behavior, and the dramatic impact of the 2020/2021 Covid-19 pandemic on countries across the world. Paulo Freire would have had something worthwhile to say about many of these developments, and his ethical, political, and educational ideas offer helpful starting points in allowing others to comment on such changes. There are also important continuities in economic and social policy from the time of Freire's death to the present day. The persistent influence of neoliberal ideas in shaping policy agendas is one obvious example. In the later part of his life, Freire was highly critical of the ethics of the market, and he would have found little from the last quarter of a century to alleviate his concerns. Educational trends already in evidence in Freire's lifetime have also continued to leave a mark. Freire highlighted the dangers of technocratic thinking in education, and this has by no means disappeared. There is still, in many educational contexts, an obsession with methods and a focus on the 'how' rather than the 'why' of teaching and learning. Examples of banking education are likewise not difficult to find. Indeed, in some parts of the world they have become more prominent as governments push aggressively for higher rankings in international tests of educational performance. An ethos of competition, within and between countries, continues to prevail, against the emphasis on cooperation, dialogue, and unity in Freire's theory and practice.

This book is being published in a series devoted to complicated conversations, and Freire's work lends itself well to consideration in this light.[1] Indeed, Freire has often served as a focal point for the interplay of different voices in educational studies. From the 1970s to the 1990s, he faced questions from conservatives, liberals, Marxists, feminists, and postmodernists, among others. Educationists with a primary focus on questions of ethnicity, colonialism, and culture also had much to say about Freire. Freire was subject to critique by some who felt he should

---

1 The idea of a 'complicated conversation', as employed here, arises from the work of William Pinar in curriculum studies. See further, Pinar (2006a, 2011, 2014, 2015).

have said more about the unfolding ecological crisis. His philosophical eclecticism opened him up to seemingly contradictory claims, with some suggesting, for example, that he was too heavily influenced by Marx, others claiming that he was not Marxist enough. More detailed discussion of debates over Freire's work, and his responses to the questions asked of him, will follow in subsequent chapters. Over the last two decades, theory has continued to move on, and some bodies of scholarship have become more prominent in educational studies than they were at the time of Freire's death. Posthumanist approaches to educational analysis provide one such example, and those who undertake work in this area would see some of the assumptions underpinning Freire's ontology, epistemology, and ethic as problematic. New developments in artificial intelligence also offer fresh challenges to the ways in which we conceptualize teaching and learning and understand ourselves as human beings. 'Big data' analytics are reshaping the way many politicians and policy makers define and address educational problems. These changes provide not a reason to discard Freirean ideas but rather opportunities to revisit them, with new questions to ask, new comparisons to be drawn, and new lines of inquiry to pursue. As Freire himself stressed, we must continually *reinvent* his work, taking into account the particulars of our contexts, our time, our problems and commitments.

This book has been prepared in the spirit of reinvention fostered by Freire. Freire argued that we should be open to the new while also not rejecting the old simply because it is old.[2] To this point we might add that what is sometimes promoted as 'new' often has more in common with the 'old' than is widely recognized or acknowledged. This is especially true of policies and practices in education. The so-called 'innovative learning environments' of the 21st century, for example, replicate many of the key features of open-plan classrooms in the 1970s. New labels may help in 'selling' policy reforms but from a Freirean perspective, it is important to place all educational developments in their appropriate historical, social, political, and cultural contexts. Freire's emphasis on the transformative potential of education did not mean that he was 'against' tradition. In his personal life, Freire expressed a deep love for many Brazilian traditions and customs. His passion for Brazilian food was well known. In his written work, too, there is nothing to suggest that tradition, in itself, is problematic. Freire simply did not want to place tradition in a privileged position, closing it off from potential critique. The same principle, he would be quick to point out, should apply to currently fashionable modes of thought and life. Reinvention does not mean rejecting the past and starting from

---

2 This point is made explicitly in *Education: The Practice of Freedom* (Freire, 1976) but implied throughout Freire's corpus of published works.

scratch in constructing something new; it implies respect for the insights offered by those who have gone before us but also a willingness to keep asking questions, keep inquiring, and keep moving with the times.

Freire's approach to education was forged in contexts characterized by deep social divisions. His theory of oppression and liberation emerged from his experience in working with impoverished rural and urban communities, and the often brutal realities of daily Brazilian life left a permanent mark on him. As will be explained in the chapters that follow, Freire saw liberation as a difficult and often painful process of struggle. The idea of liberation from conditions of oppression is central to his work. At the same time, and from the beginning, Freire made it plain that struggles for liberation must not ride roughshod over our regard for individual human beings. Liberation is not just concerned with the transformation of oppressive social structures; it also entails the development of key virtues such as openness, humility, tolerance, commitment, and willingness to listen and learn. Freire expressed his solidarity with those who were oppressed and did not pretend to be 'neutral' in his educational endeavors. But in recognizing that his pedagogical efforts, like all others, were political, he also demonstrated a strong sense of fairness, rigor, and balance in addressing social and educational problems. Freire had an underlying faith in the ability of human beings to transform the world – through critical, dialogical reflection and action – and he placed considerable trust in those with whom he worked. Trust does not, in Freirean terms, provide a license to do as one pleases; it carries with it a concomitant sense of care and responsibility. Underpinning all other virtues for Freire was the notion of love: love for one's subject area, for teaching and learning, and for one's fellow human beings. Freire's emphasis on the importance of these qualities is often forgotten, or pushed to one side. A pedagogy of the oppressed is not merely a revolutionary 'movement'; it is also an amalgamation of myriad smaller revolutionary 'moments'. Freire could see the value of collective action in bringing about change, but he also did not neglect the need for individual development.

The virtues to which Freire refers in his books are worth keeping in mind when considering the art of scholarly engagement. In the last decade of his life, Freire reflected at times on the contrasts between groups on the Right and Left in their political strategies and battles. He observed that those on the Right could, despite their differences, often forge a pragmatic unity with an eye on bigger goals; those on the Left, however, would sometimes become mired in a debilitating form of theoretical infighting, enabling those who already exercised considerable power to more deeply cement their dominant position. He could see that differences, instead of being regarded as a source of strength, could become an impediment to social change. Freire was a staunch advocate of robust debate but he also demonstrated that for this ideal to be upheld, virtues such as humility, respect, and tolerance must be to the fore. With the possibility of hiding behind a veil of anonymity in online forums, many of the limits that might hitherto have been applied to public discourse have been removed. Given the new forms of freedom afforded by the Internet, some have unleashed their fury, with openly expressed hatred and vitriolic attacks on others. Racism and misogyny are not uncommon. Times of crisis, including the worldwide Covid-19 outbreak, have brought out both the best and the worst in human beings. Academic discussion seldom plummets to the depths seen on social media but occasional examples of a mean-spiritedness that Freire would have found saddening can sometimes be found. This may be exhibited in more subtle ways than the raw, crude, unpunctuated expressions of anger, prejudice, and ignorance sometimes seen in online exchanges, but an underlying attitude of nastiness, with an intention to undermine, will still be there. Such cases often tell us more about the individual making the criticism than the person being criticized, but they are troubling nonetheless.

This book takes the virtues described by Freire seriously in engaging his own work. It starts from the position that while we may find some points of disagreement with Freire, much can be gained through continuing to explore and apply his ideas. In keeping with the spirit of reinvention mentioned above, the book builds on earlier scholarship while also attempting to offer something distinctive and new. There is, in the first chapter, a detailed overview of Freire's educational philosophy. This may be familiar territory for some readers, but it is worth revisiting, for every attempt to capture and convey key philosophical and pedagogical ideas in Freire's work will differ. The approach taken here is one that emphasizes both the coherence and the dynamism in Freire's thought, with some consistent core concepts but also a commitment to ongoing reflection, development, and change. With the theoretical foundation laid in this early part of the book, subsequent chapters add to existing conversations in several ways: first, through some new comparative work; second, via the Freirean analysis of policy developments and pedagogical relationships at the tertiary level; and third, through a consideration of ethical and educational questions in the light of lessons from literature. The hope is that this book will provide a number of avenues for further inquiry in the future, while also addressing educational themes, problems, and developments of interest to scholars and practitioners in the present. The primary focus is not on the advancement of new theory but on the fresh application of Freirean ideas.

Chapter One begins with a brief account of Freire's intellectual biography, highlighting some of his major educational commitments and the progression in his writing from influential early works such as *Pedagogy of the Oppressed* (Freire, 1972a) to his highly productive period of publishing activity in later life. Attention then turns to the ontological, epistemological, and ethical dimensions of Freire's philosophy and to the key elements of his pedagogical theory and practice. Freire adopts, from Hegel and Marx, a dialectical view of the world. There is, he maintains, a constant process of interaction between the 'objective' and 'subjective' dimensions of reality. The world is always 'in the making,' constantly undergoing change, and we humans are likewise beings of transformation, necessarily incomplete. Central to Freire's work is the ideal of humanization. For Freire, this means becoming more fully human through critical, dialogical praxis: reflection and action for transformation. Freire recognizes, however, that the pursuit of this ideal is often constrained by dehumanizing attitudes, ideas, policies, and practices. Education, conceived as a process of conscientization, has an important role to play in identifying and analyzing these impediments. Teaching as Freire sees it is an interventionist but not impositional activity. Teachers need to know their subjects well, prepare thoroughly for their classes, foster dialogue with and between students, and pose problems to be addressed. Freirean education is neither authoritarian nor 'anything goes' in nature; questioning, discussion, and debate are all encouraged but pedagogical dialogue also has a strong sense of structure and purpose. These ideas are fleshed out in this chapter and revisited in other parts of the book. Chapter One also considers some of the principal criticisms of Freire's work, showing, where appropriate, how Freire responded to the questions asked of him by others. Possibilities for further inquiry are identified and provide the impetus for investigation in the chapters that follow.

There is a well-established tradition of critical comparative analysis in Freirean scholarship. This is not what we ordinarily think of as 'comparative education,' where the focus is mainly on differences and similarities between countries in their educational policies and systems. The reference here is to comparisons between Freire and other thinkers. Over the years, Freire has been compared with scholars from many different academic fields and disciplines but also with novelists, dramatists, political activists, and religious sages. One figure who has, to date, largely escaped notice in these comparisons is the Danish philosopher Søren Kierkegaard. After a long period of relative neglect by the international philosophical community, Kierkegaard is finally achieving the recognition he deserves, and in the last two decades there has been a resurgence of interest in his life and work. Kierkegaard and Freire differed in many ways but some surprising connections can be made between their ideas. Chapter Two pays particular attention to the educational significance of doubt as a key theme in the work of both thinkers. In his *Philosophical Fragments*, Kierkegaard, through his pseudonym Johannes Climacus, draws attention to the potentially debilitating and destructive effects of doubt on both teachers and learners. The work of Paulo Freire is helpful in responding to the problems posed by Kierkegaard's account. It is argued that in Freire's pedagogical theory and practice, doubt has both epistemological and ethical significance. It is linked with other key Freirean virtues such as humility and openness, and it forms part of the process of learning how to question. It is also related, through the Freirean idea of being 'less certain of one's certainties,' to the ethical priorities we determine, the political commitments we have, and the actions we take as we negotiate our way in the world.

Earlier in this Introduction reference was made to both new developments and continuities in the decades following Freire's death. Neoliberalism was named as an example of the latter. It is important to note, however, that neoliberalism, as enacted in policy, has always been an 'impure' doctrine: a mix of various economic and social ideas, applied in distinctive ways in different contexts. Chapter Three elaborates on this observation, showing how neoliberalism has persisted – and indeed, extended its reach across the globe – while also continuing to evolve, taking on new forms. Neoliberalism has demonstrated a degree of elasticity over time, with adaptations tailored to suit different political regimes. But this only goes so far, and at one end of the neoliberal spectrum there is very little room to move. Freire expressed concern at the rigidity demonstrated by those who favored a 'pure' market approach to policy reform. He was especially disturbed by the fatalism and arrogance built into some neoliberal worldviews, calling into question the assumption that this was the only realistic and sensible way forward. He argued otherwise, showing the value of contemplating and exploring economic and social alternatives. Freire's work renders the ontological heart of neoliberalism – the self-interested, utility maximizing, perpetually choosing individual consumer – problematic. His epistemology is also fundamentally at odds with the commodification of knowledge under neoliberalism, and his approach to education differs substantially from the performance-driven models that prevail today. Chapter Three develops these points in relation to higher education policy reform in New Zealand, but there are lessons to be learned from this country that are relevant to other contexts.

The focus on higher education in Chapter Three finds further development in Chapter Four, where attention turns to a rarely considered aspect of Freire's work: his views on thesis supervision. The principles that might underpin a distinctively Freirean approach to supervision (or 'advising,' as Freire calls it) can be drawn from a holistic reading of his many published writings, but he also addressed this topic directly in a chapter of his book, *Letters to Cristina* (Freire, 1996). The suggestions made in that chapter complement his more detailed reflections on higher education in other books (e.g., Escobar et al., 1994; Freire & Shor, 1987). From a Freirean perspective, supervision is a transformative teaching and learning process. The virtues to which reference has already been made are central to the relationship between a supervisor and a student or candidate. Supervision is built on an ethic of trust and responsibility. Supervisors who respond to Freire's suggestions will have a strong sense of care for those with whom they work. Attentiveness to a student's strengths and weaknesses will be important. A thesis should be demanding, and discipline will be needed if the work is to be rigorous and insightful. Completing a thesis is an academic exercise, but it is also more than that; it should change the way a student views the world. In the competitive domain of contemporary academia, thesis students are sometimes regarded, implicitly if not explicitly, as revenue and research generating units. A Freirean approach to supervision offers a clear alternative to this kind of thinking. Freire's observations on the art of advising thesis students have important implications for broader debates over the purposes of higher education and are thus worthy of further consideration.

Chapter Five builds on the idea of a 'complicated conversation' by addressing some of the major points made in a thoughtful reading (Margonis, 2003) of an earlier book on Freire (Roberts, 2000). The primary focus of the discussion is on what might be called 'dilemmas of difference'. The chapter responds to questions raised about some of the key ethical and epistemological assumptions that lie behind Freire's work. It highlights some of the dangers of creating a binary opposition between 'Western' and 'non-Western' modes of thought. It shows how Freire differs from Plato in the way he understands knowledge and knowing, and demonstrates the importance of openness and respect when considering cultural practices that differ from our own. Freire's position on tradition is discussed in more detail, and the adoption of Freirean ideas by indigenous scholars in education is noted. The need for solidarity among different groups committed to social justice is stressed. It is acknowledged that some aspects of Freire's work remained underdeveloped at the time of his death. In this chapter, as in others, the significance of key Freirean virtues in scholarly engagement is reinforced.

There is now a substantial body of scholarship that demonstrates the potential value of literature for philosophical and educational inquiry.[3] The final two chapters build on this tradition via the work, firstly, of Albert Camus and, secondly, of Freire's countryman, Lima Barreto. Camus's novel *The Plague* has long been regarded as a classic of 20th century literature but with emergence of the world Covid-19 crisis in 2020, the book has attracted a host of new readers. The situation described in *The Plague* (Camus, 1960) bears some uncanny resemblances to the current global pandemic. There is illness, and death, on a large scale. A town

---

3   See, for example, Catton (2019), Edwards (2019), Hobson (2017), Kline and Abowitz (2020), Laverty (2014, 2019), Nelson (2008), Pinar (2006b), Roberts (2012, 2015), Roberts and Saeverot (2018); Saito (2021), Santos (2017), Schwieler (2017), Sichel (1992), and Siegel (1997).

becomes isolated from the rest of the world. There are bureaucratic delays, denials, and impediments. Hospitals struggle to cope with the influx of patients. Many businesses have to close. Families are unable to join their dying loved ones. There is bewilderment, fear, and anger. At the same time, and of significance from a Freirean point of view, there are examples of courage, commitment, and selflessness. These virtues and others are to the fore in the actions taken by the central character of the novel, Dr Bernard Rieux. In Rieux, this chapter argues, we see a model of quiet leadership consistent with the ideals espoused by Paulo Freire – an approach to working with others in a time of crisis that differs markedly from the examples provided by some world leaders during the Covid-19 pandemic.

Lima Barreto was, in many respects, a tragic figure. He experienced hardship and discrimination as well as personal and family difficulties. When he died in 1922, he had barely reached middle age. Despite these challenges, and while holding down a full-time clerical job for much of his adult life, Barreto was remarkably productive as a writer. He published both fictional and non-fictional work. Chapter Six analyses his best known novel, *The Sad End of Policarpo Quaresma* (Barreto, 2011), in the light of Freirean ideas. *The Sad End of Policarpo Quaresma* is, in part, a subtle social critique, but it is also a nuanced examination of human fragilities. Particular attention is paid to the ethical and educational problems posed by Barreto's central character. Policarpo goes 'mad' but in some respects he is more forward-thinking and sane than others who make him the object of scorn and ridicule. He is a complex fictional being who does not fit neatly into any one category of consciousness. We can, in keeping with Freirean principles, adopt a compassionate stance in reflecting on this fictional character's experience, and yet, there are no easy ethical or educational answers when responding to Policarpo's madness. The case of Policarpo Quaresma prompts us to reconsider the nature of humanization, and to ask searching questions about the limits of critical education.

CHAPTER ONE

Philosophy, Pedagogy, and Practice

The Work of Paulo Freire

The work of the Brazilian pedagogue Paulo Freire has been extraordinarily influential. Freire's ideas have been taken up not just by educationists but also by scholars and practitioners in a wide range of other fields, including theology, philosophy, sociology, politics, nursing, counseling, social work, rehabilitation studies, disability studies, and peace studies. In educational circles, Freire is regarded as one of the founding figures of critical pedagogy. He is best known for his adult literacy programs in impoverished communities, his service as Secretary of Education in São Paulo, and his classic early text, *Pedagogy of the Oppressed* (Freire, 1972a). As a writer, he was particularly prolific in the last ten years of his life. This chapter provides a brief overview of Freire's life and publications, discusses key elements of his philosophy and pedagogy, identifies some of the principal criticisms of his work, and suggests some areas for potentially fruitful further inquiry. The intention here is to lay the broad theoretical foundation for more detailed discussion of specific Freirean themes and ideas in the rest of the book.

Paulo Freire: A Brief Intellectual Biography

One of four children in a middle class family, Paulo Reglus Neves Freire was born on 19 September 1921 in the city of Recife, the capital of the state of Pernambucu in the northeast of Brazil. His mother was a seamstress. His father had served in the Brazilian army and was subsequently employed by the Pernambuco Military Police but was forced into early retirement with arterial sclerosis (Kirylo, 2011, pp. 4–5). When Freire was ten, his family, struggling under the effects of the Great Depression, moved to Jaboatão. Freire had learned to read and write at an early age, the outdoors serving as his classroom, but hunger took its toll on his performance at school. As his family's circumstances improved, so too did his results. Freire's grasp of the Portuguese language was such that he found himself, while still a secondary school student, taking on a teaching role with others (Schugurensky, 2011, p. 15). While attentive to matters of linguistic structure and syntax, he was motivated more by the beauty of the written word and its connection to the lived realities of learners (Freire, 1996).

Clearly predisposed to teaching as a vocation, Freire nonetheless did not take up this calling immediately. His initial university studies were in Law, notwithstanding his emerging philosophical and educational interests. As a young man, Freire suffered bouts of depression, later linking these to the death of his father in 1934, among other significant events in his adolescence (Freire, 1994). In his early twenties, Freire married Elza Oliveira, from whom he was to learn much that would inform his work as an adult educator. Freire's time in the field of law was short-lived, and he went on to a position with the Social Service of Industry (SESI), a role that sharpened his understanding of class differences. His political consciousness was honed further through his involvement, with Elza, in a radical Christian movement committed to the principle of social justice through the liberation of oppressed groups (Roberts, 2000).

Freire returned to university, completing a doctoral thesis with a focus on adult literacy. His distinctive approach to work in this field was already gaining attention and he was asked to lead the Cultural Extension Service at the University of Recife. In 1963 he was appointed Director of a national literacy program. He and his co-workers were highly successful in enabling adults to acquire basic reading and writing skills within a matter of weeks or months (after as little as 40–45 hours of teaching contact time), in part because Freire fostered a strong link between the written word and the world of the participants. The opening up of opportunities for the development of a more critical understanding of Brazilian society did not go unnoticed, and when the military seized power in 1964 Freire was regarded as a threat and was forced into exile. He spent five years in Chile, working with adults in a cultural extension program under the auspices of the Chilean Agrarian Reform Corporation. He completed his first book during this period: *Education: The Practice of Freedom* (Freire, 1976). (This work also appears under the title *Education for Critical Consciousness*.)

In 1969 Freire received an invitation to serve as a scholar in residence at Harvard University, and in that capacity completed the two essays that would become *Cultural Action for Freedom* (Freire, 1972b). In 1970 he took up a role with the World Council of Churches in Geneva, Switzerland, where he was to stay for a decade. With the publication of *Pedagogy of the Oppressed*, Freire's life as an educationist would change forever. The book created an almost immediate impact and would go on to become one of the biggest selling and most frequently cited scholarly works in the field of Education. Its groundbreaking significance continues to be widely acknowledged today (Darder, 2018; Jover Olmeda & Luque, 2020; Kirylo, 2020). *Pedagogy of the Oppressed* (Freire, 1972a) was released at a time of growing unrest among educational and social commentators. It was one of several 'subversive' educational texts published in the late 1960s and early 1970s – other examples included Postman and Weingartner's (1971) *Teaching as a Subversive Activity*, Ivan Illich's (1971) *Deschooling Society*, and Paul Goodman's (1971) *Compulsory Miseducation* – and generated much discussion and debate. Freire was in high demand as a speaker throughout the 1970s. He also served in consultancy roles for adult education programs in Guinea-Bissau and São Tomé and Príncipe. By the end of the decade, the political tide in Brazil was starting to change, and in 1980 Freire was able to return to his native country.

During the 1980s he was busier than ever, with academic responsibilities as a university professor, continuing requests to visit other parts of the world, and involvement with the Brazilian Workers' Party. Freire was a supporter of Luis Inacio Lula da Silva ('Lula'), who would later become President of Brazil. After a slower period in his writing career, with just two key works in the decade from the mid-1970s to the mid-1980s (Freire, 1978, 1985), Freire gained renewed momentum in the published development of his ideas through a succession of dialogical co-authored books: *A Pedagogy for Liberation* (Freire & Shor, 1987), *Literacy: Reading the Word and the World* (Freire & Macedo, 1987), *Learning to Question* (Freire & Faundez, 1989), and *We Make the Road by Walking* (Horton & Freire, 1990). Another collaborative work based on a series of dialogues in the 1980s with a group of Mexican academics, *Paulo Freire on Higher Education* (Escobar et al., 1994), would be released in the 1990s. These works were based on conversations between the authors, prompted by specific educational questions and later edited and organized thematically for publication in book form. They were, in their structure, style, and substance, broadly consistent with the pedagogical principles Freire had espoused in earlier books, though each volume had its own unique characteristics. The book with Ira Shor, *A Pedagogy for Liberation* (Freire & Shor, 1987), was especially important in highlighting some of the educational, ethical, and political challenges faced by teachers who attempt to enact Freirean ideas in First-World contexts.

At the end of the 1980s, Freire took another significant step in his educational career, accepting a role as Secretary of Education in the municipality of São Paulo. This was a major undertaking, with run-down schools and grinding poverty in many of the urban educational communities for which Freire was responsible. Some significant gains were made during Freire's tenure as Secretary (O'Cadiz, Wong & Torres, 1998; Weiner, 2003), but Freire was by this stage keen to return to his writing and he resigned from his position in 1991.

The productivity that had characterized Freire's scholarly output in the late 1980s continued in the 1990s, with a flurry of writing activity. Freire's second marriage, to Ana Maria Araujo (after Elza had died in the 1980s), was significant in allowing him to enhance and extend his intellectual work. Ana Maria (Nita) was a formidable intellectual in her own right, and her notes in some of Freire's later publications provide a valuable resource for other scholars. *Pedagogy of the City* (Freire, 1993) reflected on Freire's work as Secretary of Education; *Pedagogy of Hope* (Freire, 1994) was a revisiting of ideas, questions and criticisms raised in response to *Pedagogy of the Oppressed* (Freire, 1972a); *Letters to Cristina* (Freire, 1996) fleshed out elements of Freire's educational biography and philosophy; and *Pedagogy of the Heart* (Freire, 1997a) addressed connections between pedagogy and politics. Freire's views were also captured in a number of notable shorter pieces, including a dialogue with Donaldo Macedo published in *Harvard Educational Review* (Freire & Macedo, 1995) and a chapter in *Mentoring the Mentor* (Freire, 1997b), an edited collection devoted to his work.

Seemingly at the height of his intellectual powers, Freire died of heart failure on 2 May 1997. He had been a smoker for much of his adult life, regretting this in his later years as he contemplated the consequences his habit would have for his health and longevity. Freire's work continued to live on, with the posthumous publication of several books over the next two decades: *Pedagogy of Freedom* (Freire, 1998a), *Teachers as Cultural Workers* (Freire, 1998b), *Politics and Education* (Freire, 1998c), *Pedagogy of Indignation* (Freire, 2004), and *Daring to Dream* (Freire, 2007), and *Pedagogy of Solidarity* (Freire, Freire, & Oliviera, 2014). In these publications Freire addresses questions relating to the work of teachers, the process of inquiry, educational virtues, ethics, politics, and neoliberalism, among other key themes. In the last decade of his life, Freire had deepened, extended, and reworked aspects of the theory first developed in *Pedagogy of the Oppressed*, and had pushed his thinking in new directions with the prompting of his co-authors and scholarly collaborators. As was noted in the Introduction to this book, interest in his work has shown no signs of diminishing, with numerous books, chapters, and articles on Freirean themes having been published in the years following his death.

The Ontological, Epistemological, and Ethical Basis to Freire's Thought

Freire's approach to education is underpinned by a complex ontology, epistemology, and ethic. Over the course of his writing career, Freire drew, to varying degrees and in different ways, on a range of intellectual traditions: liberalism, humanism, phenomenology, existentialism, Marxism, radical Catholicism, critical theory, and postmodernism.[1] He was an eclectic but systematic thinker, weaving insights from others with his own ideas to build a coherent educational theory. He demonstrated a willingness to listen to others, modifying, reinterpreting, and adding to his ideas over time. He was prompted by his own reflections, by constructive criticism, and by changes in Brazilian and world politics. There would, he discovered, be no shortage of new problems to address as policies and practices changed. If Freire's work is examined holistically, it is not difficult to identify a number of key principles that remained consistent across his corpus of published writings. At the same time, and in keeping with his ontological position, there is a certain 'unfinished' quality to his work, an openness that allows others to continue building on his legacy. There is no one best way to characterize his theoretical orientation, but Stanley Aronowitz's (1993) description of Freire as a 'radical democratic humanist' provides a helpful starting point.[2] This implies a synthesis of different bodies of work and in particular signals the integration of the philosophical with the political in Freirean pedagogy.

The concept of humanization lies at the heart of Freire's work, linking the different elements of his philosophy, politics, and pedagogy together. Humanization as Freire understands it is a process of becoming more fully human, and this has both ontological and historical dimensions (Freire, 1972a). It is ontological because it is essential to what it means to *be* human. It is a 'vocation'; something we are all meant to pursue. But humanization takes place in a social context; it is pursued not in isolation, or merely as an intellectual process, but through our actions, with others, in the world. Humanization is thus also an historical vocation.

1　On the different dimensions of Freire's thought, see Mackie (1980), Mayo (1999), Morrow and Torres (2002), Peters (1999), Roberts (2000), Schugurensky (2011), and Webster (2016).
2　The reasons for favoring this 'humanistic' reading of Freire are made clear in Reveley (2018). See also Rocha's (2019) discussion of Freire's personalism.

Humans have a distinctive ability to see themselves in an historical light. As temporal beings, we can look back at the immediate or more distant past, ponder the present, and imagine possible futures. We are fundamentally *creative* beings, shaping history and culture while also being shaped by the structures, policies, practices, and ideas of the past and present. As human beings, we also have the ability to reflect on our activities in ways that are not evident, to the same degree or in the same ways, elsewhere in the animal kingdom (Freire, 1976). We can ask questions, pose problems, and consider consequences. We can wonder how the world might be otherwise and take steps to change what we see and experience. From a Freirean perspective, we remain unfinished beings, always in a process of becoming. We never reach a point where we can say we are 'complete' as human beings; there will always be more work to do.

Freire's concept of humanization was informed by his reading of Hegel and Marx, by phenomenologists such as Husserl and humanists such as Erich Fromm, by the Frankfurt School of critical theory, and by elements of existentialist thought. From Hegel and Marx, Freire adopted a dialectical understanding of the nature of reality. He accepted the key Hegelian notions of contradiction, negation and change, but emphasized, following Marx, the relevance of these ideas not just for the realm of consciousness but also for the material world (McLaren, 2000; Torres, 1994a). For Freire, it is the dialectical relation between consciousness (thinking, feeling, and willing) and material reality (both 'natural' and 'social') that is crucial from an educational perspective. Through the constant interaction between these two spheres, change occurs. We form ideas, or experience emotions, or will ourselves to do something, and act on the basis of these inner promptings to change material reality. But the reality we create, and constantly recreate, also 'acts back' on us, shaping patterns and possibilities for thought. Freire is clear, however, that while we may be 'conditioned' by material structures, policies, and practices, this does not mean we are ever fully *determined* by them (see Freire, 1997a, 1998a). He wants to retain a notion of critical human agency, while also acknowledging (with Marx) that some groups play a more powerful and prominent role than others in shaping how we understand ourselves, others, and the world.

How do we become more fully human? For Freire, it is through engaging in critical, dialogical *praxis* (Mayo, 2004; Roberts, 2000). The classic account of praxis in Freire's work is to be found in *Pedagogy of the Oppressed* (Freire, 1972a). There, Freire speaks of praxis as reflection and action upon the world in order to transform it. Reflection is a form of inner cognitive activity that is more than mere conscious apprehension. Reflection may be prompted by curiosity, or by a troubling incident, or via a deliberate effort to address a problem. Reflection is never a completely solitary process; it is always, even if only indirectly, social in nature. We learn to reflect through our interaction with others and the world. Our existence as social beings bears on both the content and the manner of our reflection. As a concept, reflection integrates two apparently opposite tendencies: movement and stillness. To be reflective demands a certain calmness, an ability to wait patiently, and to pay attention. Reflection is a kind of contemplation, and yet, for Freire it is more than that. We can remain calm in the middle of a literal or metaphorical storm (the latter might include situations of great distress, social discord, violent verbal or physical clashes, the pressure of workplace demands, or any number of other turbulent scenarios). In a world that never fully sits still, reflection can anchor us, direct us, and focus our intellectual and emotional energies. But reflection must be constantly renewed. As we act on our reflections, changing the world in doing so, we are faced with a transformed reality that itself demands further reflection. This is not a linear, mechanical process but a dynamic one, with a continuous, often subtle and unnoticed, interplay between reflection and action. Reflection, then, is also a form of movement.

Action is pivotal to our development as human beings and is an essential element in the process of transformation. To act is to harness the capacities we have as physical, intellectual, and emotional beings. Action, like reflection, sets us in motion. It allows us to test ideas, express our creativity, and become agents of historical change. Given the circumstances with which he was dealing in his work as an adult educator, action for Freire was closely connected with politics (see Findsen, 2007; Freire, 1972a, b, 1976). In the northeast of Brazil, Freire witnessed malnutrition so severe that children suffered permanent damage to their cognitive faculties. For many communities, access to healthcare was difficult. Safe drinking water would often be in short supply. Educational opportunities were limited. Those who were deemed illiterate could not vote, and were thus denied the most basic form of political participation. In both urban and rural areas, workers were often exploited and mistreated. Merely talking about these problems was not enough; this would amount to nothing more than 'verbalism' (Freire, 1972a). Political action was needed, and this, Freire recognized, would pose enormous challenges. Freire advocated not mere reform, which would leave the underlying political structures intact, but radical, revolutionary change. He was a radical in the sense that he wanted to go to roots of the problems he observed and experienced. He was not naïve about the obstacles that stood in the way of this kind of change. In rural communities, landowners would fight to maintain their control over peasant workers. In urban environments an emerging class of corporate elites would push aggressively to keep wages low. The conservative wing of the Catholic Church would also seek to preserve the status quo. Political change would, he realized, involve a long-term, multifaceted process of struggle.

To impede others in their pursuit of humanizing praxis is dehumanizing. Evidence of dehumanization was all around Freire as he lived and worked in Brazil. He argued, however, that while dehumanization was an historical reality it was not something we had to accept as inevitable (Freire, 1972a). Dehumanization is manifested, in concrete terms, through oppressive structures, policies, practices, relations, and ideas. Freire saw oppression as a key epochal theme of the 20th century, with a concomitant epochal task of liberation. Liberation, Freire made plain, is never simply given; it emerges through critical, reflective, dialogical action. Liberation demands struggle and sacrifice; it involves work and effort, across the lifespan and on multiple fronts. It is politically difficult and existentially draining; indeed, liberation is often intimately connected with suffering and despair (Chen, 2016; Roberts, 2016). Liberation is not an end-point to be reached by individuals; it is an ongoing, social process. There is never just *one* liberation movement, and in striving for the goals that matter most to us at any given time, it is important to recognize that priorities may alter as we continue to reflect on ourselves and the world around us. The notion of 'movement' itself is significant, signaling not just a collective effort to address shared concerns but a willingness to *keep moving*.

While the struggle against oppression is one of the defining features of Freire's approach to liberation, this on its own does not capture adequately what he means by the term. Liberation also entails the development of key virtues, the most important of which is *love*. It is possible to see Freire's entire life's work as a pedagogy of love (cf. Darder, 2002, 2003; Flecha, 2013; Fraser, 1997). Freire's particular interest is in a kind of 'armed' love that grapples with the complexities of social, cultural, and political change. From Che Guevara, Freire adopted the principle that love is a revolutionary virtue (see Freire, 1972a; McLaren, 2000). Love is commitment, care, and respect in our relations with others. It arises from our recognition that we are all engaged, each in our own ways, in a process of trying to make sense of ourselves and the world in which we live. In the field of education, love is significant in other ways as well. Teachers demonstrate love in the way they work with students, and scholarly activity demands a love of our domains of study.

Other virtues of importance for the Freirean notion of liberation include humility, openness, tolerance, trust, hope, and political commitment. Humility arises from the recognition that there is always more to learn. It is also connected with our ability to see in ourselves, as in others, frailties and weaknesses, and to accept these imperfections as part of the human condition. Openness is necessary if we are to make the most of the learning opportunities that present themselves to us (cf. Toh, 2018). To do so, we need to be able to trust those with whom we work. Tolerance, which does not mean giving up the right to express one's own views, is required if we are to hear what others have to say and respond with a sense of fairness and equanimity. Hope is an expression of the human capacity to struggle and to strive, to imagine and build better worlds. A world characterized by oppression and despair does not cancel out hope; it gives it its reason for being. Without political commitment, the dream of social transformation cannot occur.[3] These virtues, and others, will be discussed in more detail in subsequent chapters.

Freire's epistemology builds on his ontology and ethic. Knowing for Freire is not a form of isolated, individual, abstract, purely cognitive activity. It is social and practical in nature, and it involves not just the intellect but feelings and the body as well (see Borg & Mayo, 2000; Freire, 1996, 1998a). Knowing emerges and continues to develop as we interact with an ever changing world. Knowledge thus remains necessarily incomplete (Roberts, 2000). In addition to the virtues discussed above, Freire identifies a number of attributes specific to the process of knowing. Knowers are curious, restless beings, always open to further learning. They adopt an investigative and inquiring frame of mind when addressing a question, issue, or problem. Knowing takes effort; it requires discipline and persistence. Knowers probe and prod, often in places neglected by others or in ways that are novel and creative. Knowing is a risky process. It can be destabilizing and upsetting. It can throw up contradictions and tensions that hitherto had remained submerged or unacknowledged. As knowers, we must be able to pay attention, maintaining our focus on the object of study while also retaining a certain distance from it (see Freire & Shor, 1987). Knowing involves a willingness to not only accept, but actively embrace, a degree of uncertainty in our lives. Those who are, as Freire liked to put it, 'too certain of their certainties,' often impede the process of knowing not only for themselves but for others as well (cf. Freire, 1997a).

Freirean Pedagogy

The critical and dialogical elements of humanizing praxis come to the fore in Freire's integration of educational theory with pedagogical practice. The reflective, critical character of Freirean praxis is embodied in the complex and controversial notion of *conscientization*. Freire first employed this term (in its original Portuguese form as *conscientização*) in the late 1960s. He did not invent the word but he was the most prominent thinker to adopt it. In *Education: The Practice of Freedom* (Freire, 1976) Freire explains conscientization by reference to different modes of consciousness that had prevailed among particular groups at given times

---

3   See further, Eringfeld (2021), Freire (1972a, 1997a, 1998b, 2007), Nieto Ángel, Maciel Vahl and Farrell (2020), Roberts (2010, 2016), Roberts and Freeman-Moir (2013), and Rossatto (2005).

in Brazil's history. Magical (semi-intransitive) consciousness, dominant in rural peasant communities, was associated with a kind of resigned acceptance of social problems. The focus was very much on hand-to-mouth survival. Among such communities, difficulties experienced in daily life would often be attributed to 'God's will' or fate or destiny. Naïve consciousness, common among the new urban populations that emerged in Brazil in the 20th century, accepted the importance of change, but only of a reformist kind. The emphasis among these groups was on polemics, performance, and appearances rather than careful historical or structural analysis. Critical consciousness, the mode of thought to which Freire himself was committed, is characterized by depth in the interpretation and addressing of problems, a willingness to engage in dialogue, and a readiness to accept the new without rejecting the old simply because it is old, among other qualities (Freire, 1976). Freire did not intend these different modes of consciousness to be seen as fixed, sequential steps or stages in a linear process of individual change (Roberts, 2000). Nor did he want conscientization to be regarded as a kind of educational silver bullet that could somehow solve all social problems. Frustrated by what he regarded as frequent examples of misunderstanding, Freire stopped using the term *conscientização* for some years, but retained the ideas of cultivating an informed conscience (Liu, 2014) and developing a critical orientation toward the world as fundamental aims of education.[4]

In *Pedagogy of the Oppressed* (Freire, 1972a), Freire draws a distinction between two opposing approaches to education. Banking education relies on a one-way, monological process of transmission from a teacher to students. Teachers are expected to listen passively and to receive and accept the content of the teacher's narration without question. Knowledge is seen as a gift possessed by teachers, to be bestowed upon – banked into – ignorant students. Freire was strongly opposed to banking education and offered an alternative in the form of problem-posing education (sometimes called authentic education or liberating education). Problem-posing education begins with the assumption that both teachers and students have something important to contribute to an educational situation. It builds on, but does not rest with (i.e., endorse uncritically), the knowledge and experience students bring with them to any educational setting (cf. Shor, 1980). Knowledge is regarded not as a neutral, static body of information and skills to be passed on from an all-powerful teacher to waiting students; rather it is seen as something that is actively constructed and contested. The focus is on the posing and addressing of

---

4   For a recent discussion of how critical consciousness has been interpreted and applied in a range of empirical contexts, see Pillen, McNaughton, and Ward (2020).

problems rather than the issuing of answers. Questioning, critique, and debate are encouraged. Dialogue becomes central to the pedagogical process.

Problem-posing education is not the same as problem-solving education. Freire's support for the former had an ontological, epistemological, and political grounding. In seeing human beings and knowledge as necessarily incomplete, as always in a process of becoming, Freire recognized that while one problem was being addressed, others would arise. Moreover, the deep social injustices that provided the backdrop for Freire's work in Brazil did not lend themselves to easy, quick-fix 'solutions'; they required long-term, ongoing political work. Freire also wanted to signal the educational importance of the very act of seeing something as a problem to be investigated. This process is itself a subversive act in a world where some ideas have become so deeply entrenched that they are seldom questioned. This does not mean all things – all implied or overtly expressed ideas – must be questioned all the time. This is, of course, an impossibility, in both theoretical and practical terms. For some ideas to be questioned, others must simultaneously be accepted. And in day-to-day pedagogical practice, there is only so much time that can be devoted to given activities. Teachers and students will always need to prioritize their efforts, deciding which areas of study warrant deeper investigation than others.

Problem-posing or liberating education is not a 'method' but an approach or orientation to education built on a distinctive understanding of human beings and the world (Freire, 1987, 1997b; Macedo, 1997; Roberts, 2000). It is possible to identify key principles or features or themes in Freirean pedagogy – e.g., the development of key virtues, or the commitment to dialogue, critical consciousness and humanizing praxis – but these cannot be reduced to a 'method' or a list of methods. Freire warned repeatedly against the dangers of attempting to transport ideas uncritically from one context to another. Methods, he insisted, should not become universal prescriptions but must be determined according to the particulars of a given situation. What methods are selected will depend on who is being taught, by whom, for what, when, where, and why.

The defining feature of banking education is not 'teacher talk' but its authoritarian nature. Freire stressed that banking education forms part of a wider oppressive social system, where the interests of some groups are favored over others (see further, Beckett, 2013; Jackson, 2016; Roberts, 2000). In explicitly or implicitly suppressing difference and dissent, and in denying the possibility of critical agency in the co-construction of knowledge, banking education dehumanizes both the teacher and the students. Banking education treats students as objects rather than knowing subjects in the learning process. It is manipulative and controlling in character. It is not, however, the presence of a teacher who speaks and students who listen that in itself makes banking education oppressive. A university lecture need not be an example of banking education (see Escobar et al., 1994; Freire & Shor, 1987). Listening does not have to be passive acceptance.[5] The key is active engagement with the ideas, whether this is via speech or quiet critical reflection or writing, or in some other way. Liberating education is not an 'anything goes' affair; it must, Freire argues, have a strong sense of structure, direction, and rigor (Freire & Shor, 1987; Horton & Freire, 1990; Roberts, 2000; Tan, 2018a).[6]

While Freire did want to break down traditional barriers between teachers and students, this did not mean he saw no differences between them in their respective roles and responsibilities. He was emphatic that he was a teacher and not merely a facilitator (Freire & Macedo, 1995). A teacher, he pointed out, can exercise authority, and *be* an authority, without becoming authoritarian. Teachers have a responsibility to know their subject domains well. They need to prepare thoroughly for classes, provide an organizational structure for the courses they teach, and give some guidance on reading material. Teachers also need to know when to intervene in an educational dialogue in order to allow further productive dialogue to proceed (Freire & Shor, 1987). Teachers should alert students to competing perspectives in addressing complex topics, and they should always be open to having their own ideas challenged by the students with whom they work. This does not mean, when addressing contentious problems and issues, that teachers cannot hold a view themselves. What should be avoided, Freire maintains, is the imposition of the teacher's view, or any other, as if there is only one legitimate position that can be adopted (Escobar et al., 1994; Freire & Faundez, 1989; Roberts, 2000, 2010).

For Freire, the idea of 'neutral' education is an impossibility; teaching and learning are always ethical and political activities.[7] This is so in multiple respects. At a global level, international organizations such as the OECD and ranking systems of the kind exhibited by the PISA process play an important role in shaping national educational agendas. Multinational corporations mold patterns of behavior and consumption that bear on everyday educational life (e.g., in the use of digital technologies, the Internet, and social media). Within individual countries, the political nature of education is evident in the laws that govern what can and cannot be done in institutions such as schools and universities, in the decisions

---

5   It is important, however, to acknowledge another perspective on passivity and education. Bojesen (2018) provides an insightful account of 'passive education' as the education that occurs 'whether we attempt it or not' (p. 928).

6   For one perspective on competing accounts of the role of directiveness in Freire's work, see Chambers (2019).

7   There is an extensive literature relevant to this point. See, among other sources, Benade (2012), Freire (1985, 1987, 1998a, 1998c), Giroux (1983, 2010), Horton and Freire (1990), Mayo (1997, 1999), McLaren (1999), Roberts (2000, 2010), and Veugelers (2017).

made and actions taken by politicians, and in the policies that are produced. Questions about what to include and exclude from the curriculum, what should be read, how students should be assessed, and how they should be taught are all political in nature. The physical environment of an educational setting can also have an important influence on what becomes possible in pedagogical terms. At an individual level, teachers and students will always bring with them a set of assumptions, beliefs, attitudes, and ideas about how the world is structured, what it means to be a human being, what we should strive to achieve, and so on, all of which will play a part in giving each educational setting its distinctive character. For Freire, education does not just have political 'aspects'; it *is* a form of politics (Freire & Shor, 1987; Shor, 1993). Claims that education is or can be or should be 'neutral' or 'apolitical' are, he suggests, either naïve or disingenuous. Indeed, such claims often form an important part of the political strategy in battles over curriculum content and pedagogical practice.

Freire's work as an adult literacy educator played a pivotal role in shaping these ideas. When he was making his mark in this field in Brazil, the dominant pedagogical approach was banking education and the content that formed the heart of most literacy initiatives was largely disconnected from the everyday realities of the students. Freire offered an alternative way of thinking about literacy and the purpose of education. His starting point was to learn as much as he could about the lives of the adults who would be learning to read and write. From this initial research, a rich picture would be built up of family and working life for participating communities. Freire was interested not just in what people did to make their way in the world but how they did it and why. He wanted to know how people understood themselves and their relations with others. He listened to expressions of hope and despair, conveyed in distinctive ways by different participants. With these key themes and features of daily life in mind, Freire and his co-workers developed a set of 15–18 generative words. The first word would always be trisyllabic. Thus, in an urban area, participants might begin with a word such as *favela* (slum) or *tijolo* (brick). By breaking the word down into its syllabic parts and recombining the consonant with other vowels, a host of new words could be generated: *loja* (store), *juta* (jute), and so on. Dialogue between participants on nature, culture, human relationships, reflection, and learning was encouraged. This element of the program was regarded as an integral part of the process of learning to read. The intent throughout was to maintain a close connection between 'word' and 'world,' enabling participants to not only acquire basic reading and writing skills at a rapid rate but also to deepen their understanding of the society in which they lived.[8] Freire was open about the politics involved in this process, noting that other approaches were similarly non-neutral, but paid a heavy price for this when the military swept to power in Brazil.

In later work, Freire continued to develop the idea of a critical integration of 'word' with 'world,' applying the principles that had underpinned his Brazilian and Chilean adult education initiatives to other contexts. In discussing university reading requirements, for example, he spoke of the importance of allowing a text to both challenge and be challenged. We should, with due humility and openness, be prepared to not only ask questions of what we are reading but also to allow the author's ideas to question us. An author may prompt critical reflection by offering new ideas, or by disrupting our usual patterns of thought and categories for understanding. Freire's position was one of 'fighting' with a text while 'loving' it (Freire & Shor, 1987). He encouraged readers to link the texts they engage with social, political and cultural concerns in their own time and place. Freire acknowledged the importance of balancing breadth with depth in reading (Roberts, 2010). Breadth is necessary if we are to grasp how and where the ideas in one text might be placed in relation to a broader intellectual tradition. But depth is vital if we are to make the most of what a book can offer to us, searching, reflecting, analyzing, discussing, comparing, applying. In his own teaching, Freire would sometimes spend several weeks on just a few pages of text, and in his own reading he would often become utterly immersed in a book for hours at a time (Freire, 1996; Freire & Shor, 1987).

From an early age, reading opened up new worlds for Freire, and the outdoor environment of his immediate childhood was, quite literally, his classroom. He learned to read under the shade of the mango tree at his home (Freire & Macedo, 1987). Freire supported the reading of works by a diverse range of authors, including many that would often be marginalized in university courses, but he also believed it was important for students to encounter the 'classics' in their field. He speaks, for example, of the need to read Marx's work, regardless of whether one accepts or rejects a Marxist theoretical framework (Freire & Shor, 1987). Well-written, rigorous scholarly texts offer an opportunity for dialogue, not just with those who study them in groups (e.g., in a university class), but, indirectly, between the reader and author of a work and with the others with whom one associates elsewhere in life. Texts should, Freire showed, live with us, informing the way we think about ourselves, the decisions we make, the way we interact with others, and the actions we take. Reading critically and well is demanding but rewarding. It is

---

8 See Bee (1980), Freire (1976), Lankshear (1993), Roberts (2000), Taylor (1993), and Vahl (2018).

both a political process and an aesthetic experience and it plays an important role in our formation as ethical beings.

True to his own ideas, Freire remained a restless soul right up to the time of his death. As is clear from his later publications, he was, in particular, deeply troubled by the destructive impact of neoliberal policies in Brazil (Freire, 1994, 1996, 1997a, 1998a, 2004, 2007). Neoliberalism, whatever form it takes in a given context, stands opposed to almost every aspect of Freirean pedagogy. Neoliberals focus on individuals as self-interested, competitive, choosing consumers. Freire stresses that we are social beings. He argues against actions motivated purely by self-interest, and he is heavily critical of cultures of relentless consumption. He favors cooperation, communication and collegiality over competitive individualism. Under neoliberalism, knowledge becomes a commodity, with the same properties as other goods and services in a market. Knowledge becomes important not for its own sake, or for the role it can play in addressing social injustices, but for its exchange value (Roberts, 2004). There is, from a neoliberal perspective, no need to distinguish between knowledge and skills or information. Indeed, for neoliberals, there is a separation of the 'knower' from 'knowledge'; the latter can exist without the presence of the former. For Freire, knowing is part of the wider process of humanization, and the idea of reducing knowledge to a figure that can be listed on a balance sheet is an absurdity.

In institutions governed by neoliberal principles, there is an obsession with measurement and performance. From a Freirean point of view, the very act of trying to measure everything is itself dehumanizing. Freire's work shows that when we reflect deeply on what matters most in education, the language of measurement is unable to help us. How, Freire might ask, can we 'measure' love, care, courage, commitment, humility, and hope? Any attempt to do so diminishes the pedagogical possibilities in these terms and denies their philosophical complexity. Neoliberals support 'free' trade, and education is expected to adhere to that principle; Freire would have wanted to have seen *fair* trade, ultimately under a different mode of production, with education playing a key role in preparing people to critically evaluate the structures that might facilitate or impede this. In a neoliberal world, economic goals dominate; for Freire, prosperity and individual or corporate advancement should be secondary to the cultivation of human virtues and the struggle to overcome oppression. In the West, neoliberalism has emerged as a form of late capitalism, interwoven with the broader process of globalization. Freire saw capitalism as intrinsically 'evil' (Freire, 1998a) and held on to a dream of democratic socialism that would render the world less discriminatory, exploitative, unequal, and unjust (Freire, 1993, 1996, 2007). He saw neoliberalism as a fatalistic discourse: a way of thinking that denied the possibility of alternatives to global capitalism and denuded education of its humanity and hope (Freire, 2004; Roberts, 2010; Tiainen, Leiviskä, & Brunila, 2019). Through his writing, speaking engagements, and other activities, he fought hard to resist the tide of neoliberal reform, aware that this would be a long term battle to which many would have to contribute.

Criticisms, Responses, and Possibilities

While acclaimed by many, Freire has also attracted his share of his criticism. Over the years, he responded to many of the key questions raised by others, while also leaving open a number of areas of inquiry for further investigation. In his dealings with critics, he worked hard to apply the principles he espoused in his writings. When faced with a view contrary to his own, he would try to avoid a defensive or reactionary posture and instead, in a spirit of equanimity, pay careful, respectful attention to what was being said. He reserved his sense of moral outrage and indignation (Freire, 2004) for the brutalities of neoliberalism, maintaining a stance of openness and humility in seeking to learn more through engaging the critiques of others. At times, tensions emerged even with friends and colleagues (see, for example, Freire & Faundez, 1989) but these were for the most part productive in allowing Freire and his partners in dialogue to work through complex, contested ideas. In the early years following his rise to international prominence, critics focused principally on Freire's openly political approach to education, his style of writing, his manner of dealing with the process of class struggle, and his concept of conscientization. Later critiques paid particular attention to questions relating to cultural differences, gender, and some of the key virtues espoused by Freire. Freire has also been criticized for his apparent lack of engagement with the emerging ecological crisis.

Freire's response to the charge that he was making education political has already been signaled; he would draw attention to the ways in which it has always been thus, demonstrate the value of clarity and honesty in understanding and declaring one's politics, and reinforce the importance of allowing and fostering alternative points of view. He would also show that commitment to a specific political goal or group or movement should never override the need for rigor and balance in the teaching of curriculum content (cf. Freire, 1987). Freire's style of writing also did not please all. Some saw the language employed in *Pedagogy of the Oppressed* as too abstract or too 'revolutionary' in flavor. Freire was aware, however, that a degree of abstraction was necessary if he was to give complex philosophical ideas their due. The notion of seeing something as 'revolutionary' in the content and style of *Pedagogy of the Oppressed* was consistent with Freire's intentions (even if his concept of revolution might have differed from that embraced by some of his critics) and also reflected the contexts that had shaped the book. But he was also at pains to point out that he was not interested in a kind of sloganizing where rhetoric would stand in for sound argument and theoretical substance.[9] Freire's use of the male pronoun in his early works, with 'he' standing in for 'he or she,' was also criticized. This practice was common at the time, but Freire could see that it was problematic and, in the dialogical books of the late 1980s and throughout his writings in the 1990s, adopted more inclusive language (see further, Freire, 1997b). Frequent references to Marx and Marxists can be found in Freire's earlier publications. Even so, Freire found himself under attack from some who saw his emphasis on dialogue and the virtues associated with it as naïve when dealing with the realities of class struggle (see Freire, 1985). Freire, while attentive to and respectful of these criticisms, was at the same time disturbed by any suggestion that a process of revolutionary change should, in the interests in overthrowing class oppression, ignore the importance of human communication and voices of difference.

A well-known early critique of conscientization was mounted by the sociologist Peter Berger (1974), who saw Freire's depiction of different levels of consciousness as patronizing and paternalistic. Berger argues that Freire was committed to a process of 'consciousness raising,' where an elite group of intellectuals would lift the oppressed masses from their ignorance. He claims that Freire's approach to conscientization relies on the flawed idea that one person can be 'more conscious' than another. The problem with Berger's argument is that it attributes to Freire an understanding of consciousness, conscientization, and education that is inconsistent with the views conveyed in the Freirean texts available at that time. Freire supported the idea of people becoming more *critically* conscious, not 'more conscious' in general. Freire's early writings convey a much more nuanced, dynamic, dialectical view of consciousness than that implied by Berger's account. The epistemology that underpins Freirean pedagogy is premised on the idea that no one is fully ignorant nor fully knowledgeable. Knowing is never complete and our consciousnesses are always changing as we interact with others and the world. Conscientization is better understood not a matter of 'consciousness raising' but as continuous, subtle, ever shifting reflective process (Roberts, 2000). Others participate in shaping us as conscious beings but no one can 'raise' someone else's consciousness as if mechanically lifting it up from one relatively fixed, stable state to another. Freire's emphasis on the importance of humility, listening, and respect, his

---

9   This is evident in the following works, among others: Freire (1985, 1994, 1997a), Freire and Faundez (1987), Freire and Shor (1987), and Horton and Freire (1990).

condemnation of the authoritarianism of banking education, and his support for dialogue as a fundamental pedagogical principle also do not square with Berger's implied portrait of an arrogant, all-knowing group of educationists or intellectuals intent on converting others to their truth.

In some of the work Freire published following Berger's critique, notably his book *Pedagogy in Process* (Freire, 1978), there are perhaps more serious grounds for concern. There, Freire leaves himself more exposed to charges of intellectual vanguardism (see Walker, 1980). He also adopts, from Amilcar Cabral, the highly problematic notion of 'class suicide' (see Mayo, 1999). But the importance of contextualizing an author's work must again be stressed. The substantive heart of *Pedagogy in Process* is a series of letters from Freire to influential figures in Guinea-Bissau in a situation of revolutionary change. It is true that Freire does seem to imply, in a number of publications, that there is a 'correct' way of thinking. But when that language is examined in its appropriate contexts, it is clear that being 'correct' in those cases means being *critical* (Roberts, 1999a). Applying his own ideas on the impossibility of neutrality, Freire would be happy to admit that he does have a preferred ethical position, and that he favors some modes of thinking and being over others. When invited to serve as a consultant in a country such as Guinea-Bissau, or to lead a literacy program in a country such as Brazil, he cannot begin from a 'blank slate'; his work will be shaped and informed by his existing knowledge and experience, his hopes and dreams, his limitations. All organized forms of education, whether in kindergartens, schools, universities, or other contexts, involve *intervention* in the lives of others. But a crucial distinction can be drawn between intervention and *imposition*, and Freire's opposition to the latter is clearly evident in his work.[10]

This point has particular relevance in responding to claims that Freire's pedagogy, if applied in non-Western or traditional societies, would constitute an act of 'cultural invasion' (Bowers, 1983). Freire had no intention of entering such contexts uninvited, let alone of imposing a narrow 'Western mind-set' on the inhabitants of these societies. There is no one Western way of thinking or living or being, just as there is no single 'Eastern' worldview, culture, or system of social organization. Freire accepted some ideas advanced by Western thinkers but rejected others. He valued dialogue and the posing of problems, for example, but rejected the ethos of individualism associated with some bodies of Western thought. He was not 'against' tradition but rather sought to uphold what was best in both established

---

10 Compare, Escobar et al. (1994), Freire (1994, 1997a, 1998a, b, c), Freire and Shor (1987), and Roberts (1999a, 2000, 2010).

cultural practices and new forms of social life (Freire, 1976; Roberts, 2000, 2010). These points are developed more fully in Chapter Five.

Questions have also been raised about the concept of love advanced by Freire in *Pedagogy of the Oppressed* (Freire, 1972a). Nel Noddings (1991), for example, problematizes Freire's account of the different roles played by oppressors and the oppressed in the process of liberation.[11] She notes that Freire sees a certain power in the weakness of the oppressed, and that he believes the oppressed must, through an act of love, liberate both themselves and their oppressors. Noddings asks: 'What in the history or the experience of the oppressed leads us to suppose that they will be loving? Or is liberation an act of love simply by virtue of its result?' (p. 161). In response to Freire's urging of oppressors to take a radical stance and join with the oppressed in solidarity, she says: '[C]learly the oppressor can only approximate this solidarity. The oppressor will of necessity have a different consciousness from the oppressed and different instruments to express outrage' (p. 161). Freire's call for an 'act of love' instead of 'pious, sentimental, and individualistic gestures' on the part of the oppressor (cited in Noddings, 1991, p. 162) leaves Noddings dissatisfied: 'A full description of this 'act of love' is not forthcoming, nor does Freire justify his belief that men can or will produce such acts' (Noddings, 1991, p. 162). A danger in rejecting 'individualistic gestures,' as Noddings sees it, is that the oppressed will be reduced to an abstract category. '[B]y failing to treat in any depth the whole range of loving human activity,' Noddings argues, Freire 'risks the success of his project' (p. 163).

This line of argument is connected with a broader concern expressed by some theorists about Freire's approach to questions of difference. Weiler (1991), for instance, argues that Freire does not pay adequate attention to the multiple layers, tensions, and contradictions that characterize relations of oppression and liberation. Freire, it is said, relies on a universalist account of oppression, with a binary opposition between 'oppressors' and 'oppressed.' This ignores the fact that a man may, for example, be oppressed by a landowner or a capitalist but also *be* an oppressor in the way he treats his wife and children. When such criticisms were raised with Freire, he accepted that he may have said less about oppression along ethnic and gender lines, while explaining that his principal focus was class oppression (compare, Freire, 1997b; Freire & Macedo, 1993). Where Freire did comment on matters of gender, he sometimes did himself no favors, and this remains a weakness in his work (cf. Jackson, 2007; Mayo, 1999). While Freire himself said relatively little about questions of ethnicity, race, and indigenous education, other

---

11 The relationship between violence and love in *Pedagogy of the Oppressed* can also be questioned. For a recent example, see Wilcock (2020).

scholars have found much of value in his work in addressing these areas of inquiry (see, for example, hooks, 1993; Murrell, 1997; Smith, 1999).

Noddings is right that in *Pedagogy of the Oppressed*, Freire's account of love leaves some unanswered questions. But Freire urged his critics to read beyond *Pedagogy of the Oppressed*, and to recognize that his ideas had evolved and developed over time. In later books, he spoke at some length about love from an ethical, political, and educational point of view. He reinforced his abhorrence of sexism and racism – indeed, all forms of discrimination (see Freire, 1993) – but also noted that people were not *just* characterized by their differences. He argued for a position of unity in and through diversity (see Freire, 1996, 1997a, b, 1998a), primarily on ethical grounds but also for pragmatic reasons. He was aware that while differences often exist among those on the political Right (e.g., between economic liberals and moral conservatives), such groups would often forge a strategic unity when facing opposition from the Left. Achieving this kind of unity would sometimes prove difficult if not impossible for those on the Left, who would be unable to work productively with their differences and would (figuratively speaking) tear themselves apart through theoretical infighting.

Freire felt that differences should become not antagonistic to dialogue but essential for its existence. For without something to provide contrast or tension there is no movement in an educational conversation. It is not a matter of 'overcoming' differences but rather of working constructively with them (cf. Rozas Gomez, 2007). The very existence of complexity, tension, and conflict between groups in educational situations can itself become an object of critical inquiry. This is not to deny imbalances in the way power can be exercised in given situations. To the contrary, Freire maintained: relations of power (including those between teachers and students) must be confronted and addressed. But this, for Freire, does not mean dialogue between individuals and groups who differ along class, gender, ethnicity, and other lines is impossible (cf. Ellsworth, 1989). Just as no group gathered for an educational purpose (or for any other reason) can be without differences, so too will there never be a situation where those present have nothing in common. Quite apart from any specific features that bind a group together (e.g., all being committed to learning in a particular subject domain, or all having been present during a significant event, or all feeling dissatisfied in some way with their work), there is, from a Freirean perspective, something that unites us all as human beings: our vocation of humanization – our universal human ethic, as Freire referred to it in his later work (Freire, 1998a).

Freire's appeal to a position of unity in diversity remained an inadequate response from the point of view of many of his critics. Indeed, the term 'diversity' might be seen by some as indicative of the shortcomings in his approach.

'Diversity' is not the same as 'difference.' Many who had serious misgivings about Freire's work on oppression and liberation drew on postmodern, poststructuralist and post-colonial currents of thought. In his later books Freire does refer to postmodernism, speaking of it as an attitude of openness and linking it with his idea of not becoming too certain of one's certainties (see Freire 1994; Peters, 1999). He aligns himself with 'progressive' postmodernism, emphasizing the importance of remaining committed to the process of political struggle and social transformation, whatever our differences, in the face of the enormous challenges posed by neoliberal policies and practices. But he did not address questions of postmodernism and postmodernity in a detailed way.

There are other bodies of work that could have been helpful in fleshing out some key elements of his pedagogical theory. Freire speaks frequently of the importance of feelings, as well as reason, in our educational development, and the theme of care is clearly important in his approach to teaching. Drawing more overtly on scholarship in the philosophy of emotion and the ethics of care, where Noddings, mentioned earlier, is a key figure, could have enhanced these aspects of his work (see further, Roberts, 2010). Freire has a great deal to say about epistemological, ethical, and educational virtues, but there is little direct engagement, in his published writings, with the wider philosophical literature in this area (e.g., virtue ethics). He also said little about the world ecological crisis that emerged as a problem of great significance in the last quarter of the 20th century, though he was, it seems, beginning to write in this area near the end of his life, and his ideas have inspired others who have worked in this domain (Gadotti, 2011; Reigota, 2013; Schugurensky, 2011).

Paulo Freire was a thinker who invited ongoing reflection and critical engagement from his readers. As noted earlier in this book, he actively encouraged educators to 'reinvent' his work in their own contexts.[12] He should not been seen as an educational 'guru' or 'hero' with 'followers' or 'disciples,' and attempts to construe Freire and/or those who engage his work in this way often say more about those applying such labels than those to whom they are applied. Freire's work has weaknesses and omissions, as is true, of course, of all significant figures in the history of educational thought. In the last decade of his life Freire was, in some respects, *too* productive, and the publication of fewer books, with more time to deepen, extend, and refine his ideas and to comment on the work of other scholars, might have addressed some of the shortcomings that remain in his educational theory. He was, in keeping with his own understanding of humanization, an

---

12 For a Freirean perspective on 'insider-outsider' tensions in different contexts, see Misiaszek (2018).

'unfinished' writer, and there is considerable scope for further inquiry in building on the openings he provides.

Putting his ideas into conversation with other thinkers, East and West, is one way of pursuing this agenda. Among the many thinkers, teachers, activists, and writers with whom he has been compared are Lao Tzu, Confucius, Plato, Jean Jacques Rousseau, Maria Montessori, Johann Heinrich Pestalozzi, G. W. F. Hegel, Karl Marx, John Dewey, Mahatma Gandhi, Rabindranath Tagore, Mikhail Bakhtin, Antonio Gramsci, Ernst Bloch, Simone Weil, Amartya Sen, Martin Buber, Emmanuel Levinas, Hannah Arendt, Che Guevara, Lorenzo Milani, Julius Nyerere, Jurgen Habermas, Hans-Georg Gadamer, Michel Foucault, Ivan Illich, Maxine Greene, Nel Noddings, bell hooks, Martha Nussbaum, and Jacques Rancière. This is not an exhaustive list.[13] Such analyses often focus as much on differences as similarities, but the range of people invoked in these comparisons is itself significant and indicative of the reflection prompted by Freire's work. Critical comparative scholarship need not be limited to those who publish non-fictional texts. A Freirean framework can, for example, lend itself well to an educational reading of novels and short stories, and productive connections can be made between Freire and literary figures such as Mary Shelley, Hermann Hesse and Fyodor Dostoevsky (Roberts, 2010, 2012; Rozas Gomez, 2013).

Neoliberal ideas, policies, and practices continue to evolve, and the concerns Freire raised in the last few years of his life (Freire, 1994, 1997, 1998a, 2004, 2007) provide starting points for others in addressing the problems posed by these developments. Several aspects of Freire's ontology, epistemology, and ethic are worthy of further reflection, including his concept of the human subject, his notion of knowing as a holistic process (involving the body, mind, and feelings), his approach to the pragmatics of political change, his theory of social class, and the nature and significance of key virtues in the process of liberation. Educators in a variety of pedagogical settings can build upon, critique, and apply ideas from Freire on the roles and responsibilities of teachers and students (see Peters & Besley, 2015). Freire's link between 'word' and 'world' (Freire & Macedo, 1987) has much to offer in theorizing literacy practices in a range of contemporary contexts. His comments on higher education (in Escobar et al., 1994, and elsewhere) have ongoing relevance for debates over university goals and priorities.

---

13 Many of the names that appear here are drawn from Schugurensky (2011, pp. 188–191). See also Beckett (2018), Benade (2015), Bingham (2016), Farrell (2018), Glassman and Patton (2014), Guilherme and Morgan (2018), Lake and Kress (2017), Mayo (1999, 2013), McLaren (2000), Morrow and Torres (2002), Roberts (2010, 2012, 2016), Rule (2011), Shim (2007), Shyman (2011), Snauwaert (2011), Tan (2018b), and Vlieghe (2018).

Conclusion

Paulo Freire has left an indelible mark on the theory and practice of education over the last half century and it seems likely that his work will continue to generate wide-ranging interest, inquiry, and debate in the decades that lie ahead of us. Freire was deeply committed to education and social justice in his homeland of Brazil, but he was also a pedagogue who, in a certain sense, transcended national boundaries. In the years following the publication of *Pedagogy of the Oppressed*, he became one of the best known and most influential educationists in the world. His legacy lies not just in the books he published but also in the actions he took as a teacher, the decisions he made as an administrator, the feelings he expressed in his relationships with others, and the intellectual problems he posed for himself and others. When Freire's contributions are examined holistically, it is clear that his espousing of a 'universal human ethic' did not prevent him from paying close attention to particulars. The myriad small moments of love, joy, anger, curiosity, pain, and persistence mattered greatly to Freire. He relished life in all its fullness, and tried to encourage others to do likewise. Taking up this invitation, in whatever ways are appropriate for different groups, in specific contexts and at given times, is a task many educationists will embrace enthusiastically.

CHAPTER TWO

Learning to Live with Doubt

Kierkegaard, Freire, and Critical Pedagogy

In his *Discourse on the Method*, first published anonymously in 1637, René Descartes stipulated that he would 'accept nothing as true which I did not clearly recognize to be so'; he would reject as false anything that might have the least ground for doubt (Descartes, 1911, pp. 92, 101). Descartes' method was to subject everything to doubt, and to see if anything remained that could be taken as entirely certain. The one proposition he arrived at that appeared to withstand this critical scrutiny was the claim, 'I think, therefore I am' (p. 101) and this formed the first principle of his philosophy. This single, short statement has become among the best known of all philosophical utterances, and has, over the centuries, generated an extensive body of critical scholarship. Rather less attention has been paid, in popular discourse at least, to the intellectual orientation that gave rise to Descartes' claim: the notion that we should begin with doubt. This starting point is arguably a matter of great educational importance, for it goes to the heart of what many in the West see as a key pedagogical aim: the development of our capacity to question received wisdom.

This chapter considers the nature and consequences of doubt from a philosophical and educational perspective, initially via the work of the Danish thinker Søren Kierkegaard. Close attention is paid to one publication in particular, *Philosophical Fragments* (Kierkegaard, 1985), where the theme of doubt figures prominently. At the time of its publication in 1844, *Philosophical Fragments* 'remained unnoticed, un-reviewed, unmentioned anywhere' (Kierkegaard, 2009, p. 4). That is not the case today, with interest in the work growing substantially over the last two decades.¹ *Philosophical Fragments* concerns itself not so much with Descartes specifically but more with what Kierkegaard refers to, somewhat vaguely, as 'philosophy' and 'modern philosophy.' It is clear, however, that Descartes, along with Hegel, is one of Kierkegaard's key targets. *Philosophical Fragments* is, in keeping with Kierkegaard's practice in several other works, written under a pseudonym: Johannes Climacus. It is important to note that Climacus is among the more skeptical of Kierkegaard's pseudonymous philosophical figures; he is less willing than Kierkegaard himself to follow the path of faith (see Hannay, 1989, p. 15). Climacus, as a doubting presence in Kierkegaard's corpus, is well placed to ask some searching questions of doubt itself.

Philosophical Fragments contains two works in one; it is the second, titled 'Johannes Climacus, or *De Omnibus Dubitandum Est:* A Narrative,' that provides our focus here. As the title suggests, the work is set out in the form of a story, but one that explores philosophical questions in detail. The central 'character' (that term applies only loosely here) is Climacus himself. Apart from one other figure – Climacus's father – others in the narrative make only vague appearances, with few details to distinguish them as characters. For all intents and purposes, then, this is a depiction of the thinking and experiences of one fictional individual, who is partly a representation of Kierkegaard's own views but not an exact match for them. Fittingly perhaps, in this book at least, Kierkegaard leaves the reader in some doubt as to his precise position on doubt. Indeed, part of the ongoing appeal of Kierkegaard's work lies in his ability to seduce the reader through humor, irony and deception, while at the same time having something serious to say in addressing philosophical questions.²

There are many different theoretical approaches that can be taken in exploring the implications of Kierkegaard's thought for education,³ but in examining *Philosophical Fragments* the work of Paulo Freire is particularly helpful. At first glance, Kierkegaard and Freire might appear to have little in common. They lived in different centuries in different parts of the world. One is best known for his philosophical and theological concerns, the other for his contributions as an educationist. They seem to have had very different personalities and purposes as authors,

---

1   See, for example, Carreño (2007), Cockayne (2015), Evans (2004), Hale (2002), Harrison (1997), Howland (2006), Kim (2012), Malesic (2007), Mercer (2001), and Nowachek (2014).
2   Cf. Berthold (2011), Evans (2004), McCreary (2011), Saeverot (2011, 2013), Sharpe (2016a), Williams (2012), Zook (2008).
3   See Hill (1966), Kwak (2001), McKnight (2004), McPherson (2001), Roberts (2016), Saeverot (2011), Tubbs (2005), and Wivestad (2011).

with quite distinct audiences. Yet, there are also some surprising connections that can be made. Kierkegaard is more concerned with pedagogical matters than the titles of his books might suggest, and Freire's approach to education is underpinned by a robust philosophical framework. Neither wanted to reduce the question of doubt to a form of methodological skepticism. Both refused to separate matters of epistemology from ontological and ethical concerns. Both employed writing as a means for working through ideas, often revisiting key themes again and again in their books. And to judge by the number of publications devoted to their work over recent years, both seem to have much to offer 21st century readers.

In *Philosophical Fragments* there is an implied theory of doubt as a pivotal aspect of educational experience, evident in the thoughts, words, deeds, and relationships that structure Climacus's tale. Kierkegaard allows the reader to see how doubt is cultivated, how it is taught and learned. He also draws attention to the potentially debilitating and destructive effects of doubt on both teachers and learners. In Freire's pedagogical theory and practice, doubt is linked with virtues such as humility and openness, and it forms part of the process of learning how to question. But it is also related, through the Freirean idea of being 'less certain of one's certainties,' to the ethical priorities we determine, the political commitments we have, and the actions we take as we negotiate our way in the world. A key problem posed by Kierkegaard's narrative is the question of whether the discomfort and distress created by doubt can be justified. Freire does not offer an easy, quick-fix 'solution' to this problem but he does help us to appreciate why the cultivation of doubt should not be separated from other elements our educational formation. By placing individual subjective experience in its wider contexts, he also reminds us that doubting is a shared, social process. Both Kierkegaard and Freire show that whether we are comfortable with the consequences of doubt or not, once we go down the path of critical education, there is no going back. We keep developing and changing but we cannot completely or permanently 'switch off' the voice of doubt. Instead, we must learn to live with the prompting of a critical consciousness, albeit in different ways in different contexts. The first section outlines Climacus's experience of doubt as depicted in *Philosophical Fragments*; the second section addresses some of the key educational problems posed by Kierkegaard's account in the light of Freire's ideas.

Learning to Doubt

Climacus learns about doubting by watching others. We are introduced to him as a young, introverted student in his twenty-first year. Preferring a life of seclusion to one of outward success or prominence, Climacus is in love not with a woman but with thinking. He experiences great joy when he is able to form coherent, higher thoughts; he feels despondent and oppressed when his thinking pushes back against the coherence he desires. The movement of thought, he discovers, is imperfect, and this distresses him. An explanation for Climacus's apparently unusual conduct – he appears as a 'stranger in the world' (Kierkegaard, 1985, p. 119) – can be found in his earlier life. His father, we are informed, was a strict man, and Climacus was granted few opportunities to become distracted with matters beyond the home. At times, his father would offer him the chance for a walk, which Climacus accepted. The walk was not outside but up and down the floor within the house. What might have been perceived as an inadequate imitation of the 'real thing' became for Climacus an exercise in the development of the faculty of imagination – a quality his father possessed in abundance. Climacus's school experiences complemented the informal education he received from his father at home, with Greek grammar proving particularly productive in transporting his mind to more distant open spaces. In tandem with the development of his growing imagination, Climacus also acquired a sense for that which is sudden or surprising. Here too his father was his principal teacher, demonstrating through arguments with others the power of listening carefully, allowing others to say all they wanted to first, and then dismantling everything that had been said with just a few carefully chosen words.

Returning to the present, we learn that Climacus, now at university, is still quiet and withdrawn but nonetheless willing to seek out like-minded others. It is philosophers with whom he connects. He is attentive when others speak, and he reflects carefully on what they have to say. He feels he is not yet sufficiently profound to become a philosopher, but he is determined to continue with his thinking. When he runs into difficulties in thinking through a problem, he wills himself to see it through and experiences great pride when he was successful in doing so. His travels, not lacking in adventure, have all been in his mind; all he needed to venture anywhere in the world was a room and a window. He dwells in the realm of ideas but he is disturbed by his father's growing depression. Having gradually come to the view that his father is extraordinary, Climacus is also troubled by his lack of jest, his 'gloomy earnestness' (p. 125). His father's skill in dialectical reasoning and argument – his ability to reduce an opponent to speechlessness – leaves Climacus feeling uneasy: 'His formative influence was not a man who knew how to propound his knowledge as valuable but was instead one who knew how to render it as unimportant and valueless as possible' (p. 125).

As more of Climacus's tale is told, we learn that despite being a student, he finds reading uncomfortable and does little of it. When he is tempted to pick up a book, he often discovers that his thoughts become disrupted and matters are left undecided in his search for answers. He finds the authorial practice of outlining and refuting the views of others tedious and irritating and misses 'the wonderful sport of dialectic, its puzzling surprises' (p. 130). He eventually gives up reading, blaming not the books themselves but his upbringing for making him different from others. He retains his capacity for listening and pays special attention to the idea that 'Everything must be doubted' (p. 131). Climacus sees this thesis as his central task if he is to become a philosopher. In listening to others, he formulates three main claims regarding the connection between this thesis and philosophy: '(1) philosophy begins with doubt; (2) in order to philosophize, one must have doubted; (3) modern philosophy begins with doubt' (p. 132). He does not address these in order, beginning instead with the last claim.

With insufficient reading or training to investigate further, Climacus accepts the last premise as true. The next question then becomes: Was it by accident or by necessity that modern philosophy began with doubt? After much deliberation, he finds he cannot answer that question adequately, and this pains him. He cannot decide whether the third thesis is identical with the first one. He does not find any help in the company of others, noting that in conversations, different people would use different theses but believe that they were 'saying the same thing' (p. 139). Others are not bothered by their lack of precision in testing these ideas but Climacus is unable to adopt such an attitude himself. He remains 'restless and troubled' (p. 140).

Climacus tries to let his thoughts work on him with all their weight, distinguishing the 'laboriousness of thinking' from 'the weight of the thought' (p. 141). He makes a determined effort to bear the weight of an historical thought, but is overwhelmed by it and faints. When he regains consciousness, he can barely turn his attention to the thought. He sees that unless one has very strong nerves, this kind of thinking could lead to madness (p. 141). He sinks into a state of discouragement but as he does so, he finds, almost against his will, that a kind of clarity emerges. This too, however, proves fleeting. He wants to declare that the third thesis is an impossibility but he does not have the courage to do so; his investigation has cost him much 'time and hard work' and he has been 'poorly rewarded for his troubles' (p. 143).

Turning his attention to the first thesis, Climacus notes that if philosophy begins with doubt, it begins with a negative principle. An alternative approach was exhibited by the Greeks, who taught that philosophy begins not with doubt but with wonder. Wonder, Climacus observes, is an 'immediate category and involves no reflection upon itself'; doubt, by contrast, is a 'reflection-category' (p. 145). Those who begin with wonder establish a continuity with the Greeks but when the starting point for philosophy is doubt, this continuity is broken, for 'doubt is precisely a polemic against what went before' (p. 145). Climacus also points to a problem that arises when one person states the first thesis in the company of another. If the other agrees with the claim, he or she is simultaneously expressing disagreement with it, for to agree that philosophy begins with doubt is not to doubt at least that proposition. Climacus's state of mind is such that he cannot adhere to philosophical principles merely for the sake of consistency. He has other questions that demand answers.

Following his deliberations, Climacus is unsure whether doubting is a form of preparation. The process of investigating doubt has left him feeling old before his time, the innocence of youth having been taken away from him. He concludes that he must do everything on his own, taking full responsibility as he continues to pursue the second thesis. Having taken on this task, he first allows the thesis to work on him, deep within, surrendering to the thoughts and moods that go along with this. Aware of the profoundly individual nature of his searching, he is still curious to find out how others have fared in setting out on the same task. He is distressed to discover that among other philosophers little seems to be said about the fate that awaits those who attempt to doubt everything (p. 164). The few comments he does pick up from a philosophers prove woefully inadequate. Dejected, he decides to leave philosophers behind forever, and to follow a method of making everything as simple as possible.

Living with Doubt: The Unsettling Process of Education

Kierkegaard did not construct *Philosophical Fragments* as an overtly educational text. This is not, on the face of it, a book 'about' education; nor, so far as we can determine, were Kierkegaard's motives in telling Climacus's tale explicitly or exclusively pedagogical. Kierkegaard's pseudonymous authorship and use of irony should dissuade us from seeing *Philosophical Fragments* as a didactic work. This does not mean, however, that nothing of value for educational theory can be taken from the text. Climacus's tale raises questions about the process of learning, the nature of knowledge, and the roles of teachers and students in pedagogical situations. These questions arise as Climacus ponders the central theme of doubt. Kierkegaard leaves the reader 'hanging' in searching for definitive answers to these questions, and that is, in part, why reference to others can be helpful. Paulo Freire was one of the most influential figures in the development of critical pedagogy (Kirylo, 2013) and his work continues to be widely read today. Freire places a premium on the value of 'learning to question' (Freire & Faundez, 1989), and questioning is often prompted by the existence of doubt. Doubt for Descartes is a methodological matter, but for Freire, as for Kierkegaard and other thinkers such as Miguel de Unamuno (see Evans, 2013; Sartwell, 1991; Unamuno, 1972), it has much deeper ontological and ethical significance. Freire does not 'solve' the pedagogical problems introduced by Climacus's account but he does offer some educational ideas that are helpful in continuing the conversation started by Kierkegaard. His distinction between 'authority' and 'authoritarianism' is particularly important in this respect, as will be argued later in this section. First, though, attention must be paid to the place of doubt in Freire's work, and this requires some reference to the social and political conditions that prompted him to speak out on these matters.

In his later years Freire frequently conveyed the view that we should not be too certain of our certainties (Escobar et al., 1994; Freire, 1994, 1997a). His development of this idea was, in part, a response to what he saw as the excessive certainties of neoliberalism, where it was assumed that there was only one reasonable, realistic approach to social and economic organization. Neoliberals, Freire felt, were too closed and too fatalistic in their thinking (Freire, 1998a). They were unable, given their zealous adherence to the ideology of the free market, to imagine, let alone develop and pursue, alternative modes of social and economic life. They were anti-utopian and could not conceive of 'better worlds' beyond a narrowly circumscribed set of possibilities.[4] Being less certain of one's certainties entails the adoption of a posture of greater openness – openness to other ideas, other perspectives, other ways of understanding human beings, other ways of living in the world. Doubt is often viewed in a negative light, as something to be avoided, but when understood in relation to the principle of openness it takes on a different character. An expression of doubt can be an indication of integrity: an honest admission that one does not know. Admitting to doubts can also signal a willingness to examine one's own views critically and to change.

Questioning may not only be prompted by doubt; it can also lead to further doubts. The 'treadmill' of perpetual doubt (Langer, 1929), with the process of doubting giving rise to further doubts, is a well-established phenomenon. From one perspective, this endless cycle of one doubt leading to another can be seen as an impediment to the pursuit of knowledge. It might be said that we are *always* in doubt about the epistemological ground on which we stand. This can be unsettling and destabilizing; it can also undermine our ability to justify claims made or actions undertaken. But the Freirean notion of being less certain of one's certainties is not the same as saying we are totally *un*certain. To be *less* certain can imply that, were

---

4   See Freire (2004, 2007), Gadotti (2017), Roberts and Freeman-Moir (2013), Walker (2009).

it not for a posture of openness and a willingness to entertain doubts, we might be *more* certain. The terms 'less' and 'more' in this context are not intended to suggest that certainty is something that can measured or quantified; determining how certain we are about something is more a matter of making a qualitative judgment (cf. Beckett, 2008). Such judgments are subject to change. We may recognize within ourselves a tendency toward greater certainty in some domains of knowledge, or in some situations, or at some times, than others. From a Freirean perspective, there is neither absolute certainty nor complete uncertainty. In practice, we take some things as given in order to form judgments, make decisions, and move on. Questioning one idea presupposes the acceptance of other ideas. The doubt that arises from questioning need not be debilitating. We can accept the fact that we will be less certain than we would like to be, and we can learn to live with the discomfort that arises from this.

But while we may learn as individuals to accommodate the intrusions of doubt into our thinking, those who are teachers must also consider the consequences of doubting and questioning for the students with whom they work. A critical, questioning consciousness, once developed, cannot simply be 'switched off.' If teachers plant seeds of doubt in what may hitherto have been unquestioned views among students, and encourage the posing of problems (cf. Freire, 1972a, 1987, 1998b), over time the critical habits of mind formed through classroom experiences become cemented as a mode of being in the world. One may try to ignore the voice of critical doubt but it is still there, making its presence felt in the myriad moments of everyday life. Students may find they can no longer enjoy some forms of entertainment as they once did; they may question their motivations and goals; they may experience considerable distress as they renegotiate their views of themselves, others, and the wider world. They may feel frustrated at their inability to adequately address the injustices they now perceive. A generally happy disposition may give way to a more somber outlook on life. There is no 'going back' in critical education, understood in these terms, and this poses serious ethical questions for teachers (Roberts, 2016; Roberts & Saeverot, 2018). In teaching others how to doubt, as Climacus's father does with his son, we must, if we care about those with whom we work, be able to justify the longer-term consequences of our actions on other lives.

Freire's 'answer' to this ethical dilemma for teachers is more implicit than explicit and can best be gleaned from a holistic reading of his work. He would have been quick to point out that while we may be guided by a set of ethical principles in our teaching, and have some idea of what *may* follow from the development of a more questioning frame of mind, we can never be certain of the consequences of our actions for others. Education is an unpredictable process, and attempts to make it less so can sometimes denude it of its value. Indeed, he would have argued that the goal of trying to establish direct 'cause and effect' connections between teacher 'inputs' and student 'outcomes' rests on an impoverished, technocratic view of education that is dehumanizing for both teachers and students (cf. Freire, 1987, 1997b, 1998a; Freire & Shor, 1987). Nonetheless, even if it is granted that students will respond in different ways to the prompting of doubt and that educational 'outcomes' cannot be predicted with certainty, this does not mean teachers should simply step back and let the process of critical transformation unfold. To the contrary, they have an important role to play in preparing and supporting students as they change. Indeed, it is not, of course, only the students who change; the teacher is also transformed through the act of posing problems and working with the students. Moreover, while there may be no 'going back' with critical education, this should not be taken to mean there is a simple, single, momentous step from one state of consciousness to another. Nor is it a matter of progressing through a series of fixed, sequential, linear, hierarchical stages (Roberts, 2000). Freire stressed that we are *unfinished* beings, always in a state of becoming, and the development of a critical orientation to the world is a gradual, ongoing process (Freire, 1972a, 1998a).

The idea of not being able to 'go back' was pivotal in Kierkegaard's conception of *Philosophical Fragments*. His plan was that Climacus would learn how to doubt, experience some distress in exercising his doubting consciousness, and discover to his horror that he could not return to his pre-doubting self. Doubt would become a primary source of despair. In other writings, Kierkegaard explored faith-based responses to despair (see Kierkegaard, 1987, 1988, 1989, 1998, 2009), but in *Philosophical Fragments* he is more ambiguous and remains ambivalent in the answers he provides to the problems he poses. While Kierkegaard does not cast his narrative in precisely these terms, the experiences Climacus undergoes can be seen as a form of critical education. Climacus learns how to doubt through his experiences at home, in school, and at university. He learns through observation, reflection, and action. His unusually 'sheltered' upbringing, with much of his time as a child being spent inside his home, means the range of activities in which he participates is rather limited, but he does not seem to resent or regret this. His concerns about the value of doubting are evident from an early age, yet doubt appears to play an important role in his scholarly development. His father's increasingly depressed countenance is particularly worrying for him, and the inference we can draw from Kierkegaard's narrative is that this may be closely related to the nature and significance of doubt in his father's life. But having been raised in an environment built on the principles of doubting, questioning, and dismantling,

Climacus finds he cannot, as concerns arise, step outside the parameters imposed by these experiences.

Climacus's approach when confronted with the uncomfortable psychological and emotional consequences of doubt is to tacitly reinforce the inner tendencies that trouble him. Unable to 'walk away' from doubt, he undertakes a philosophical examination of it. Climacus is uneasy, uncomfortable, and unhappy with the forms of doubt he sees being expressed and displayed by others and with those he experiences himself. Yet, all he can do is reaffirm the central place of doubt in his life by making it the starting point for disciplined inquiry. He cannot break out of a cycle of doubt, and even the prompt for wanting to do so – his doubts about the value of doubt – is itself based on the principle of doubting. Climacus may declare that he wishes to adopt a method of making everything as simple as possible, but Kierkegaard allows the reader to see that he is unlikely to be successful in his pursuit of this goal. There is no 'going back' for Climacus, and while he may be able to make some things simpler in his life, he will be doing so, readers are led to believe, on the basis of a more complex understanding of himself and the world.

Kierkegaard draws our attention to another pedagogical feature of doubt. Climacus is intrigued by a comment from a philosopher that his first thesis is from 'the eternal philosophy' and must therefore be embraced by anyone who becomes committed to philosophy. His initial thought that the reference to being 'eternal' may mean a fully abstract approach to philosophy, unconcerned with time, is quickly refuted by his recollection that the thesis refers to a beginning. For Climacus, the beginning in this thesis is subjective, not objective; doubt is experienced not in the abstract but by a particular individual. When one individual is viewed in relation to another, however, the essentially tragic nature of doubt is revealed. Climacus recounts an old tale of a knight and troll to illustrate what is at stake here. The knight receives from the troll a special sword that craves blood the moment it is drawn. The knight cannot resist drawing the sword, and the troll's fate is sealed. The same consequences seem to await those who embrace the 'philosophy begins with doubt' thesis: 'when one person said it to another, it became in the latter's hand a sword that was obliged to slay the former, however painful it was for the latter to reward his benefactor in that way' (Kierkegaard, 1985, p. 155). To teach another about the thesis, then, is, in a certain sense, to sacrifice oneself as a teacher. It involves being prepared to be 'slayed' by those whom one teaches, by that which is being taught. The absurdity of this process, whereby an otherwise mild mannered thinker becomes a 'bloodthirsty Bluebeard' cutting down immortal philosophers, brings both smiles and tears for Climacus (p. 156).

A clue to addressing the ethical problems posed by the cultivation of doubt through teaching lies in Climacus's response to the second of his theses. This thesis, it will be recalled, is that 'in order to philosophize, one must have doubted' (p. 157). Here Climacus begins with a recognition that in earlier times, some form of preparation for philosophy had always been necessary, whether this was in the form of silence, or obedience, or asceticism. He has little difficulty accepting this principle, believing that anything worth obtaining requires difficulty and hardship. Humility, he suggests to himself, is necessary in preparing to be a philosopher. This seems to pose a problem when considering 'teachers' and 'learners' in philosophy, for '[h]e who doubts elevates himself above the person from whom he learns, and thus there is no frame of mind less appreciated by a teacher in his pupil than doubt' (p. 158). He tries to see this from a different point of view, asking whether in encouraging their pupils in this way, teachers actually encourage greater reliance upon themselves. Students, in doubting, can come to grief and learn from this, just as a child might be taught to respect fire by being permitted to burn his or her hand. But Climacus is not satisfied with this 'learning from experience' explanation. He wonders, as an alternative, whether in positively ordering the student to do something (even if this involves questioning one's own views), the teacher is committing a noble act. The teacher assumes responsibility, and the student 'thereby becomes a less perfect being, one who has his life in another person' (p. 158). Climacus responds to his own musings by noting that by 'imposing something negative, the teacher emancipates the follower from himself, makes him just as important as himself' (p. 159). This cancels the relation between teacher and student, and this appears to be of concern to Climacus.

A key term in the above paragraph is *humility*. In his pedagogical theory, and in the way he conducted himself as a human being, Paulo Freire consistently demonstrated the importance of humility as an epistemological and ethical virtue (see Kirylo, 2011; Roberts, 2010; Schugurensky, 2011). For Freire, a posture of humility is consistent with a commitment to other virtues such as care, respect, attentiveness, reflectiveness, and openness. It was noted earlier that Climacus's father listens carefully to others when they speak, and this ability is, from a Freirean perspective, an essential attribute of both teachers and students. But for Climacus's father, listening does not seem to be coupled with humility; it is a means for grasping what is being said in order to 'knock it down.' Philosophy in contemporary contexts is sometimes like this. It can become a kind of quiet (or noisy) battleground, with each participant seeking to gain an advantage over others in a war of ideas. The object is more to 'win' than to learn, or to teach. Climacus's father might claim that he is displaying care and respect for his interlocutors through the very act of dismantling their arguments; he shows through his actions that his opponents' ideas are worthy of engagement. Freire would not have disagreed with this, but he would have added that without humility, neither participant in this form of philosophical exchange will reap its full educational value.

Humility is important in avoiding the blindness that can accompany excessive certainty about the correctness of one's own position. Humility does not 'create' doubts; rather, it allows doubts that are already there to be perceived and acknowledged. Freire spoke repeatedly against dogmatic, defensive and reactionary stances in addressing complex social, cultural, and political questions.[5] He had observed these tendencies not only among those on the political Right but also, at times, in groups on the Left. The latter he found all the more distressing, given his open support for democratic socialism. It concerned him too that while different groups on the Right could often forge a pragmatic unity in the face of opposition, those on the Left would often end up fighting over their differences, losing sight of what they had in common (cf. Freire, 1997a, 1998a, c). The Right, already substantially advantaged in the resources at its disposal, would, in the face of a heavily divided Left, find it that much easier to push through reforms that further strengthened their dominant economic position. A dogmatist is convinced of the correctness of his or her position and will not be persuaded otherwise. There is a closure, generated in part by a lack of humility, to the possibility of seeing the world otherwise. Evidence and argument will often be insufficient to dislodge the dogmatist from his or her views. For the dogmatist, doubt represents a sign of weakness and must be eliminated.

Climacus considers several different positions on the relationship between teachers and students. In the knight and troll example, the teacher sacrifices himself or herself to the student by revealing the 'philosophy begins with doubt' thesis. In later reflections, Climacus wrestles with what we might see as questions of pedagogical authority. He does not reach a definitive conclusion, instead leaving the reader to wonder whether certain forms of compulsion are necessary and justifiable given the good they will ultimately bring for students. Freire would not have denied that sacrifices are necessary in committing wholeheartedly to the process of teaching. He was conscious of the fact that teaching demands long hours, often with woefully inadequate wages, and is intellectually, emotionally, and physically exhausting (cf. Freire, 1998b). He would have been happy to say that teaching involves a form of service to others, but he would have wanted to probe the Kierkegaardian notion of sacrifice a little further. A teacher, Freire argued, can and should exercise authority, but should not be *authoritarian* (see Freire & Shor, 1987;

---

5   See, for example, Escobar et al. (1994); Freire (1972a, 1985, 1993, 1994, 1996, 1998c, 2004), and Freire and Shor (1987).

Horton & Freire, 1990). This distinction is important in understanding why Freire insisted on calling himself a teacher and not a facilitator (Freire & Macedo, 1995).

From a Freirean perspective, teachers should have a certain authority in their command of their subject matter; they should know their specialist areas well and will want to continue to deepen and extend their knowledge through further study and reflection. They will also possess a thorough understanding of different approaches to teaching. They will exercise authority by intervening in educational conversations where necessary to ensure all have opportunities to participate. Teachers facilitate dialogue and discussion, but they are not *merely* facilitators. They have an important role to play in recommending helpful reading, in posing problems for students, and in fostering the exploration of social and economic alternatives. They provide structure, rigor, and direction in learning and investigation (Roberts, 2000). A teacher cannot be neutral and will always favor some ethical ideals over others; education in this sense, among others, is a political process (see further, Freire, 1985, 1987, 1998c; Mayo, 1999; Shor, 1993). At the same time, the teacher should not *impose* his or her views on the students. The possibility of questioning what the teacher says, or how he or she acts, must always be there. An authoritarian teacher does not wish to be challenged and will often actively suppress views contrary to his or her own. Inwardly, an authoritarian teacher may, from time to time, experience doubts; outwardly, however, he or she will refuse to waver.

For Freire, learning how to question is also a matter of learning how to demonstrate humility and respect. The authority of a teacher can be strengthened rather than undermined when he or she allows doubts to form and be expressed among the students with whom he or she works. There is a sacrificial element to the pedagogical process, as Climacus signals, but what exactly is being 'given up'? A teacher committed to Freirean principles willingly sacrifices the possibility of exercising some forms of power (e.g., the power to dominate, or to manipulate, or to control), but in doing so, opens up other possibilities. Respect is generated not by attempting to crush the spirit of the other but by *giving* respect. Exhibiting a certain form of 'weakness' by allowing students to see that teachers too can have doubts is also a sign of strength. Being prepared to put one's views to the test in the company of others can allow positions to be held with greater conviction. A Freirean teacher gives up something of his or her ego but this allows him or her to pay attention to the student, and to the object of study, in ways that would otherwise not be possible.

Climacus is concerned that the teacher-student relation may be canceled out if the student becomes 'just as important' as the teacher (Kierkegaard, 1985, p. 159). It is true that Freire talked in *Pedagogy of the Oppressed* about the resolution of the teacher-student contradiction as one of the underlying ideas in problem-posing education (see Freire, 1972a). But this was in the context of a critique of 'banking education,' where an authoritarian relationship between teachers and students was taken as given. Freire's point was that teachers, if they bring to their craft an appropriate sense of humility, openness, and respect, also learn from students through the act of teaching. Students in this sense can teach their teachers. This doesn't mean, however, that there are no meaningful differences between teachers and students. As Freire stressed in later work (e.g., Freire, 1987, 1996, 1998a, b; Freire & Shor, 1987; Horton & Freire, 1990), teachers and students have certain distinctive characteristics and responsibilities, even if they also share much in common. It is not unreasonable, for example, to expect teachers to have greater breadth and depth in their understanding of the subject being taught than the students; the years of study in preparing to become a teacher should count for something in this respect. But, as Freire was fond of saying, no one is ignorant of everything just as no one knows everything (see Freire, 1976); there is always more to learn, even in the subject areas with which we are most familiar, and teaching is one of the best ways to sharpen and sustain that learning process.

Conclusion

Both Kierkegaard and Freire responded through their work, in their own distinct ways, to the specific concerns of their time and their circumstances. But they can also speak to us today. In a 'post-truth' era, with excessive certainties often based on blatant lies, the importance of doubt – of being prepared to question, despite the risks this brings – is arguably more evident than ever before. Kierkegaard may have adopted what might be seen today as a 'conservative' stance in response to the questions he posed, ultimately embracing a Christian view of the world. But his distinctive approach to matters of faith was unorthodox in his time and he suffered considerable scorn and ridicule for his manner of working and his idiosyncratic philosophical views. Kierkegaard found a faith-based answer to his doubts but this was no easy, straightforward 'conversion'; it was a risky, deeply reflective leap into the unknown. Freire's faith was important to him, but he also faced significant risks in taking the task of doubting and questioning seriously.[6] His pedagogy emerged from his practice as an educator in contexts that were demonstrably oppressive (see Freire, 1972a, b, 1976, 1985). He worked with adults who were

---

6 On the nature, role and significance of faith in Freire's work, see Byrne (2011), Kirylo and Boyd (2017), Madero (2015), and Neumann (2011).

severely impoverished, exploited by capitalists in urban areas and by landowners in rural communities. The students in the literacy programs he initiated would often have had few opportunities for education in their earlier lives. Malnutrition, ill health, and high rates of infant mortality were common. Freire was aware of the risks for him, and for the participants, in opening up the door of doubt through such programs.[7]

Doubting, both Kierkegaard and Freire show, is not a mere methodological game. It can sometimes be literally a matter of life and death. Freire did not tell the adult learners in his educational programs what to think, or how to think. Political orientations were neither prescribed nor proscribed. But Freire knew there was no 'innocent' way to encounter potentially challenging ideas through education. His approach was seen as inspiring by many, but it was also deeply unsettling. It was highly effective in enabling adults to learn to read and write but it was also concerned with more than the acquisition of skills and content. With the military coup in Brazil in 1964, Freire found himself targeted as a subversive and was forced into exile. Doubt, he discovered, could be 'dangerous' – not just for students but for teachers as well. The term 'subversive' is often employed in a pejorative sense, as a kind of stick to beat down competing political views. A teacher who is subversive is cast as someone who is unusual, extreme, not to be trusted. Yet, from a Freirean perspective, all education should, in some senses, be subversive. It should enable the foundations on which a society stands to be questioned. It should make us feel uncomfortable, slightly on edge. Education exposes us to emotional, intellectual, and (sometimes) physical risks, but without these forms of exposure, others forms of risk come into play.

Perhaps the greatest sacrifice, from an existential standpoint, made by both teachers and students is the loss of 'innocence' that comes as doubts are raised and addressed. For Kierkegaard's Climacus, this loss of innocence is experienced as a sense of unease, a disturbing feeling that all is not well. The underlying anxiety that is created through the cultivation and expression of doubt can be made all the worse by the feeling of not being able to go back. Freire had to consider whether the risk of allowing participants in his literacy programs to consider their social circumstances in a fresh light could be justified. He was satisfied that this was a risk worth taking, but he did not form this view lightly. Both Freire and Kierkegaard help us to see that even if we decide that the dangers of doubting are too great, risks remain. We risk the decay and stagnation that can come from ignorance, closed-mindedness, or indifference. Both Kierkegaard and Freire railed against indifference, albeit in very different ways. Both were passionate in the

---

7   On the risks associated with the development of a critical consciousness, see Suissa (2017).

pursuit of their ideals, and in the way they lived their lives there are some abiding lessons for other educators.

Neither Freire nor Kierkegaard would want to suggest that the teacher's task is one of 'converting' students. The integrity of the student as a knowing, doubting, questioning being must be honored. Teachers do have a role to play, however, in fostering a sense of care and commitment among students. Indifference may be feigned but it can also be tacitly encouraged. Education can assist us in identifying and analyzing how and why this might be so. Through education, ideas and ideals should come to *matter* for students. This makes life more complicated and difficult for students but it is also part of what gives educational experience its sense of excitement and promise. Coming to care about ideas and ideals connects students with others, ancient and contemporary, who have (as Climacus observes) *wondered* about themselves and the world around them. 'Wonder' does not limit itself to that which is beautiful; it can be experienced in the midst of social 'ugliness' (the oppression to which Freire referred), pain, and despair. Doubt of the Freirean kind can enhance rather than impede the development of a sense of wonder. Wonder, as the early Greeks understood it and as Freire affirmed through his work, presupposes an openness that authoritarian modes of social life deny. Doubt, as a partner with wonder, can play a crucial role in our formation of educational beings.

CHAPTER THREE

Impure Neoliberalism

A Freirean Critique of Dominant Trends in Higher Education

One of Paulo Freire's principal concerns in the last years of his life was the destructive impact of neoliberal ideas, policies, and practices on human dignity and development. In the decades following Freire's death, neoliberalism has continued to evolve, with its influence extending to a wider range of countries across the globe. In education, as in other areas of social policy, there has never been a 'pure' application of neoliberal ideas. The formation, interpretation, and implementation of educational policy is often a complex, messy, contested process, characterized by tensions and compromises between different policy actors and conflicting ethical imperatives. As such, the task of analyzing and understanding policy is never easy. Nonetheless, despite myriad variations in the extent to which and ways in which neoliberal principles have taken hold across the Western world, some persistent key themes can be identified. Of special significance for educationists are features such as these: the ontology of self-interested individualism that underpins neoliberal thought; the reliance on the model of the market as a guide when structuring educational systems; the treatment of knowledge as a commodity; and the logic of performativity that drives institutional life. In these areas among others, Freire provides a clear point of difference in examining and assessing current policy directions. This chapter addresses these contrasts with particular reference to neoliberalism and higher education reform in New Zealand.[1]

Neoliberalism and Higher Education: A Case Study

In the 1980s, New Zealand was regarded by some political figures and policy makers as a model case of neoliberal reform.[2] Following the election of the fourth Labour government in 1984, New Zealand witnessed a series of sweeping economic changes. These have been well documented over the years but are worth recalling briefly here. Industries that had previously been subject to tight government control were deregulated, agricultural subsidies were removed, and the New Zealand dollar was floated. 'Free' trade was promoted, and tariff levels were reduced. A key architect of the reforms was Roger Douglas, who served as Minister of Finance during Labour's 1984–1987 term in government. Douglas advocated rapid change, in quantum leaps, allowing little or no time for interest groups to mobilize. Prime Minister David Lange wanted to slow the pace of reform and when Labour was re-elected in 1987, he dismissed Douglas from the Finance portfolio. In the late 1980s and early 1990s, government departments and public institutions were increasingly expected to operate like corporations. A commitment was made to greater efficiency, improved performance, and thinner bureaucracies. Buffers between government and the institutions affected by policy changes were removed.

Labour was defeated by the National Party in the 1990 general election but the process of neoliberal reform continued.[3] The program of state asset sales initiated by Labour was embraced enthusiastically by the National government. National was predisposed to an agenda of further privatization, and this was implemented

---

1 In New Zealand, the term 'tertiary education' is more commonly used in policy than 'higher education.' The former is more expansive than the latter, and includes all forms of post-compulsory education (e.g., universities, polytechnics, private training establishments, indigenous institutions of higher education, industry training organizations, and adult and community education). The main concern in this chapter, however, is the impact of neoliberal ideas on universities.
2 On the theory of neoliberalism, see Harvey (2005) and Flew (2014).
3 The two largest political parties in New Zealand are the National Party and the Labour Party. These are similar in many respects to the Conservative Party and the Labour Party in the United Kingdom. Traditional distinctions between the two parties as 'right' (National) and 'left' (Labour) have been steadily eroded since 1984. Now, the tendency in New Zealand media is for National to be portrayed as 'center-right' and Labour as 'center-left,' but this masks the fact that there has been a general movement to the right of the political spectrum by both parties. New Zealand operates under a Mixed Member Proportional (MMP) parliamentary system, allowing smaller parties to exert some influence over policy via coalitions and agreements with the larger parties.

in fits and starts throughout the 1990s. A strong culture of entrepreneurialism was fostered, and National sought to extend New Zealand's reach on the world economic stage. With the introduction of the Employment Contracts Act, the power of unions was undermined and workers were required to become more 'flexible' in responding to the demands of employers. National sought to minimize state intervention in individual lives, and to place greater faith in market mechanisms as the means for distributing opportunities and resources. Where Labour had focused mainly on economic restructuring, National made its mark in the way it applied neoliberal ideas to the social policy portfolios. Government support for beneficiaries was reduced, hospitals were recast as 'crown health enterprises,' and market rates were introduced for state housing tenants. The most far-reaching changes, however, were in the sphere of education.

In universities, neoliberal ideas found administrative and organizational expression via the philosophy and practices of managerialism. The process of corporatization that had begun during Labour's second term in the 1980s was pushed forward aggressively. The Vice-Chancellor was now regarded as a Chief Executive Officer, and governance structures came to increasingly resemble those found in the world of business. Student loans were introduced, marking the beginning of debt mountain that would grow to billions of dollars within a few short years. The ethos of collegiality that had served as the bedrock of academic life was systematically undermined by discourses of accountability, the adoption of 'performance indicators,' and the reconfiguring of staff relationships along more hierarchical lines. New, more rigid, reporting requirements were set in place, and closer auditing of academic activities became the norm. Where before a culture of trust with an attendant sense of responsibility had prevailed, now there was a suspicion among some politicians and policy officials that academics could not be trusted to manage their own affairs. What needed to be avoided, it was believed, was the phenomenon of 'provider capture,' where too much control would be granted to institutions, with unacceptable risks for government and tertiary education students. 'Choice' and 'competition' became the twin pillars of the new tertiary education policy environment. The tertiary system was expected to operate as a quasi-market, with different providers competing with each other to attract educational 'consumers' to their courses and programs.

A change of government in 1999, to a Labour-Alliance coalition, ushered in New Zealand's version of 'Third Way' politics. Labour-led governments were re-elected for two further terms, and during this period two tertiary education strategy documents were released (Ministry of Education, 2002, 2006). Tertiary education was seen as a means for advancing New Zealand as a 'knowledge society and economy.' The hands-off approach that had been espoused by neoliberal reformists in the 1990s gave way to a process of government steering, with stronger state oversight in shaping a 'shared vision' for tertiary education. A more overt commitment to greater social inclusiveness, and to addressing the aspirations of Māori and Pacific learners, was evident in tertiary education policy. The heavy emphasis on maximizing choice in the tertiary education sector was reduced somewhat. At the same time, some key elements of the 1990s neoliberal agenda were pushed even further under the Labour-led years of 1999–2008. Knowledge came to be seen, more and more, as a commodity, subject to the same laws that govern the production, circulation and consumption of other commodities in a capitalist society. Competition, both between institutions and within them, intensified. The marketing of tertiary education, with each institution seeking to promote its distinctive 'brand' to prospective students from New Zealand and abroad, became more prominent than ever. The logic of performativity continued to prevail, and new systems for measuring and monitoring academics came into being (Kenny, 2017). One of the most significant initiatives was the Performance-Based Research Fund (PBRF), introduced in 2003 and still in operation today (Roberts, 2006). New Zealand's universities now compete vigorously with each other to increase their share of the PBRF, as this has become the principal source of government funding for research.

With a shift back to a National government in 2008, the push to align tertiary education more closely with the needs of industry and business became more pronounced. The government placed a high priority on the STEM subjects (Science, Technology, Engineering, Mathematics), and the humanities and social sciences were progressively devalued. Two terms employed in earlier versions of the Tertiary Education Strategy – 'relevance' and 'quality' – have found a continuing place in more recent policy documents (e.g., Ministry of Education, 2009; New Zealand Government, 2014). The National government's primary concern was to make New Zealand more competitive on the world economic stage. There was a heavy emphasis on efficiency and performance. A clear message was sent to tertiary education providers that they would need to respond more directly to labour market signals in their course and program offerings. Similar sentiments were expressed in relation to research, where the expectation was that knowledge generated in institutions such as universities would be harnessed to enhance productivity. A 'Productivity Commission' was established, with the stated aim of providing 'insightful, well-informed and accessible advice that leads to the best possible improvement in the wellbeing of New Zealanders' (New Zealand Productivity Commission, 2016, p. ii). The Commission argued that the New Zealand tertiary education system is characterized by inertia and needs to become more innovative, responsive and adaptable in meeting diverse learner needs (New Zealand Productivity Commission, 2017a, b, p. 1).

A change to a Labour-led government in 2017 has witnessed the introduction of a number of new initiatives in the sector, most notably a fees-free policy for students undertaking their first year of tertiary study. There has also been some consolidation of offerings across polytechnics, with the formation of a new body – the New Zealand Institute of Skills and Technology (NZIST) to oversee qualifications and training in this part of the tertiary sector. The aggressive push under National to more closely align tertiary education with business and employer demands is less evident under the current government. A review of the PBRF scheme has been completed (PBRF Review Panel, 2020), and a new *Tertiary Education Strategy* has also been developed (Ministry of Education, 2020). The latter is a very concise document, with goals specific to the tertiary sector integrated with a statement of National Education and Learning Priorities. The Tertiary Education Commission continues to play a powerful role in the national management of the tertiary education system, complementing the influence exerted by the New Zealand Qualifications Authority since the 1990s (Roberts, 1997; Walker, 2020). A new discourse on the importance of 'impact' is emerging, but it is unclear at present exactly what that will mean in policy terms. The Covid-19 crisis has delayed the completion of some of the intended policy work in education, but further significant changes are likely over the next few years.

Humanizing Higher Education: The Freirean Alternative

Central to neoliberal thought is an understanding of human beings as self-interested, rational, utility-maximizing, autonomous individuals. The neoliberal individual is a perpetual chooser and consumer, who seeks to satisfy his or her wants and gain an advantage over others in a competitive world. Freire's work proceeds from a very different ontological starting point. As we have seen in earlier chapters, from a Freirean perspective, we have an ontological and historical vocation of humanization (Freire, 1972a). We pursue this ideal through praxis: critical, dialogical, transformative reflection and action (Roberts, 2000). Humanization means becoming more fully what we already are as human beings, but this is not an abstract process. We humanize ourselves as beings in particular contexts, at given moments in history, with others. To impede others in this pursuit is dehumanizing. Where neoliberals focus on individuals, Freire emphasizes the social nature of human existence (Freire, 1976). Learning, from a Freirean perspective, is a dialogical, collective activity (Walker, 2009). Ultimately, Freire shows, we can never be completely alone. Even if others are not physically present with us, their influence on us remains. We are always shaped in how we think, feel, act, and relate to others by the social structures, historical practices, and cultural traditions of the worlds we inhabit. This is not to suggest that we are ever fully *determined*; for Freire, whatever our current social circumstances, change is always possible (Freire, 1998a). Freire does not deny that human beings can sometimes be motivated by self-interest in their decisions and actions but he does not see this as an innate drive. Self-interest is not inevitable, and the propensity to appeal to it is itself a reflection of the economic, social, and political systems that structure our lives. In education, as in many other fields of human endeavor, much of what we do is demonstrably driven more by an interest in the well-being of others than our own personal economic self-interest (Freire, 1998b; Horton & Freire, 1990).

Freire's epistemology also stands opposed to the neoliberal concept of knowledge. In the New Zealand context, the commodification of knowledge is one aspect of neoliberalism that has remained constant throughout the 'more market' era of the 1990s, the 'Third Way' years of 1999–2008, and the post-2008 period. Students have been encouraged to see knowledge as something to be purchased, with a view to enhancing their earning capacity. Universities and other tertiary education organizations have been portrayed as 'sellers' of knowledge, in competition with each other to package and market their products effectively as they seek to establish their distinctive niche in the market. Knowledge on this model is seen as something that can be contained, possessed, circulated, and traded. It is, for all intents and purposes, indistinguishable from information. Education has been viewed in a similar light, as a commodity with an exchange value. Thus, over the last two decades in New Zealand, 'export education' has emerged as a major growth industry. Initiatives in this area have been impeded by the global Covid-19 pandemic but are likely to emerge again as government restrictions are lifted.

The idea of thinking about knowledge and education primarily in profit-driven terms would have been repugnant to Freire. Under neoliberalism, knowers are almost incidental to the process of buying and selling knowledge. 'Knowing' is simply another form of 'having' in a neoliberal world. For Freire, knowing is a mode of being: a way of understanding ourselves, others and the world (Freire, 1985, 1996, 1998a, b). Knowledge is not a static product to be bought and sold; it is constantly in the making. Under neoliberalism, there are incentives to make the process of acquiring knowledge as easy and as rapid as possible. From a Freirean point of view, the task of knowing is demanding and difficult; it takes time, effort and dedication. It can be painful as well as joyous (Chen, 2016; Roberts, 2016).

Knowers are curious, investigative, probing beings, and they are also persistent. Against the tendency to try and 'please the customers,' a Freirean approach sees education as a process that can sometimes be unsettling and uncomfortable. An educative experience may challenge learners to question their existing wants and preferences, while opening up new possibilities for further investigation.

The logic of performativity that has become so pervasive in the tertiary education system is also disturbing from a Freirean perspective. The idea of maximizing 'performance' operates across several levels. At an international level, it is New Zealand's position on league tables that compare economic or educational performance across countries (e.g., the PISA rankings) that matters. Nationally, performance standards are set for educational institutions in meeting reporting requirements, attracting students, gaining external funding, and staying within designated budgets. The global financial crisis was used by the National government elected in 2008 as a justification for saying, explicitly, that institutions would have to do more with less (Ministry of Education, 2009). The gaining of ever greater efficiencies, with 'outputs' maximized relative to 'inputs,' has been another consistent theme across the different permutations of neoliberalism in New Zealand. Within universities and other tertiary education organizations, the language of performance also dominates. Academic staff have been placed under relentless pressure to be productive in their research, effective in their teaching, and entrepreneurial in seeking financial support for their work. Teaching is evaluated through student surveys (typically based on Likert scale rankings), allowing university management, promotions committees, and continuation review panels to reduce a teacher's value to little more than a number. Overall, academics are monitored and measured more frequently and more invasively than ever before.

Freire was not against the idea of performance *per se*. Across many of his writings, he stresses the importance of meeting high standards in academic work. He spoke regularly of the need for rigor in scholarship and teaching (see Freire, 1985, 1998a, b; Freire & Shor, 1987). He was always insistent that whatever a teacher's political commitments, he or she has a responsibility to know his or her subject well, to prepare thoroughly, and to be well organized in classroom activities. Teaching for Freire was not an 'anything goes' affair. His famous critique of banking education in *Pedagogy of the Oppressed* (Freire, 1972a) was sometimes interpreted as a license to abandon any sense of structure and discipline in the classroom. A careful reading of that work and many that followed makes it plain, however, that his alternative to banking education – problem-posing or liberating education – was a rejection not of authority but of *authoritarianism*. A teacher needs to be an authority in his or her knowledge of a field of study, and he or she needs to exercise authority in day-to-day pedagogical practice (Freire, 1987,

1997a). Teaching for Freire is, as has been noted elsewhere in this book, not mere facilitation (Freire & Macedo, 1995). Both teachers and students are important in an educational context but they are not equivalents to each other. Teachers have some responsibilities that distinguish them from students. Knowing when and how to intervene in an educational dialogue can be important, for example, in allowing all students a chance to participate (Freire & Shor, 1987). Teaching, Freire might have been happy to say, is always a certain kind of 'performance' and those who practice this art should be expected to become highly adept at it. But these ideas have little in common with performance as performativity in contemporary tertiary education policy discourse.

In reducing academic work to a series of inputs, outputs, and outcomes, all measured at regular intervals, with steps being taken to discipline those who fall short in meeting the specified standards, tertiary education is drained of its humanity. Staff and students themselves become 'outputs' and 'outcomes.' Increasingly, we are led to believe that nothing matters in education unless it can be measured in some way. Under research assessment regimes such as the PBRF, it is not only knowledge that becomes commodified but also the researchers who create that knowledge. Researchers are encouraged to sell themselves and their work, in the service of increasing revenue for their institutions through higher PBRF grades. Acceptance of the need for taxpayer's money to be well spent in the tertiary education sector does not mean systems such as the PBRF are well justified. For there are much more well-rounded ways of assessing competence and evaluating achievements (e.g., by looking at a full CV, reading an academic's work, gaining statements from colleagues and thesis students, observing him or her in action in teaching classes or serving on committees, considering community contributions, and so on). But such approaches are too 'messy,' too imprecise, too time-consuming and inefficient in the contemporary university. The notion of performance that is embodied in contemporary tertiary education policy and practice is oriented toward compliance, rather than growth and development. In this sense, it is anti-educational, and the idea of basing research on a strong culture of collegiality and support is being undermined. The whole process of preparing and submitting PBRF portfolios has become heavily systematized, and participating researchers are expected to become more machine-like in not only producing outputs and outcomes but in recording them (Roberts, 2007a, 2013). From a Freirean point of view, this is a degrading and dehumanizing approach to research.

The authoritarianism to which Freire objected in his account of teaching is now present in a more subtle form in the tertiary education sector. Authoritarianism as Freire understands it is evident in pedagogical approaches that deny the critical subjectivity of students. It can exist when a teacher suppresses questioning and critique, or discourages dialogue and discussion, or denies the possibility of alternatives when addressing complex social questions (Escobar et al., 1994; Freire & Faundez, 1989; Freire & Shor, 1987). But one might also say that there is an authoritarian character to the language of performance as exhibited in current policy. It is assumed that economic prosperity is the overriding goal for all human beings, and that tertiary education should first and foremost be directed toward achieving that end – both for New Zealand as a country and for the specific individuals who participate in the tertiary education system. The dominance of economic imperatives has become so complete that contemporary policy documents seem to be unable to offer anything of significance or substance when discussing the social benefits of tertiary education (Roberts, 2014). The notion of tertiary education serving a wider public good has all but disappeared from such documents. There is no questioning of the global economic system into which tertiary students are being ushered. The idea of considering alternatives to capitalism as a part of a tertiary education experience finds no place in this policy discourse. Creativity and innovation are permitted, even encouraged, but only if they adhere to the same basic logic underpinning all tertiary education reform over the last three decades. They must be harnessed to keep driving capitalist growth and to better position New Zealand in world economic markets. Creativity under such conditions ends up becoming conformity.

In his later work, Freire returned to the idea of humanization, speaking at that stage of a 'universal human ethic,' against which he placed the ethics of the market (Freire, 1998a). The latter, he believed, largely ignored questions of social justice, and the result, he observed in Brazil and elsewhere, was widespread inequality, poverty, and misery. He was upfront in declaring his own preference for democratic socialism and his abhorrence at the injustices of global neoliberal capitalism. Yet, while Freire was never afraid to speak openly about his own political views, he also stressed the importance of allowing alternative positions to be heard. This is a key theme in the book, *Paulo Freire on Higher Education* (Escobar et al., 1994). In that volume, Freire defends a notion of tolerance that goes beyond the mere acceptance of opposing points of view. He maintains that university teachers should not only permit but actively encourage the exploration and discussion of alternative social ideals. Tolerance, he argues, does not mean letting go of one's own ideals; to the contrary, knowing what one is committed to (and why) is a key component of a well-lived intellectual life. But what university teachers do not have a right to do is to *impose* their views on others (Freire & Shor, 1987; Roberts, 2010). University teaching is a necessarily interventionist process, but intervention is, it will be recalled from earlier chapters, not the same as imposition. The moment we step into a university classroom, we cannot avoid leaving a mark on other lives, but if we are to respect the intellectual independence of the students we teach we must allow and foster the expression and investigation of views contrary to our own. This speaks to a broader point about the politics of education.

From his earliest writings, Freire argued that education can never be neutral; teaching and learning are always political processes (Mayo, 1999; Roberts, 2000; Schugurensky, 2011, Shor, 1993). In teaching, we cannot but favor some ways of understanding human beings and the world, some cultural practices, some modes of social life, over others. Freire's concept of politics is not limited to party politics. The political dimensions of education are evident in how we teach, what we teach, and why; in the reading we select or recommend; in what does not appear in the curriculum as well as what does; in the forms of assessment employed; in the physical structures of classroom spaces; and in the views that teachers and students bring with them to any pedagogical environment. International organizations such as the OECD, the International Monetary Fund, and the World Bank have a direct or indirect bearing on educational arrangements in many countries. Multinational corporations, particularly those associated with computing and digital technologies, also exercise an influence over the tastes, aspirations, scholarly habits, and social relationships of participants in higher education. At a national level, the decisions made, laws passed, and policies formed by politicians have a substantial impact on educational lives.

Freire saw that neoliberalism was portrayed as if it was a neutral approach; the only possible sensible and reasonable solution to social, economic, and educational problems. This implied appeal to neutrality is no accident; it not only masks the politics at work in neoliberal reform but is itself an indication of those politics. By positioning opposing positions as 'old fashioned,' 'irrelevant,' or 'unrealistic,' neoliberal politicians, knowingly or unknowingly, suppress the kind of robust debate that is necessary to sustain authentic democratic life. This constitutes what Freire refers to as a 'limit situation,' requiring 'limit act' if it is to be resisted and transformed (Freire, 1976; see also, Walker, 2008). The 'TINA' principle ('There is no alternative'), often attributed to former British Prime Minister Margaret Thatcher, has become cemented in political and policy consciousness. From a Freirean perspective, however, there are *always* alternatives. This does not mean all social problems lend themselves to quick or easy solutions. Quite the opposite is true in most cases, and this is, in part, why Freire referred to problem-*posing* education as his ideal in *Pedagogy of the Oppressed*, not to problem-*solving* education (Freire, 1972a).

The problems Freire saw as an educationist in Brazil in the early 1960s – desperate poverty, malnutrition, poor healthcare, run-down living conditions, and widespread illiteracy – had deep structural roots (Freire, 1976). Education alone could not 'solve' them, and the process of addressing such difficulties would take years, not weeks or months. This does not mean education has no role to play; Freire believed that it can and should engage and address the most difficult social problems we face. But an important quality for any educationist is patience. An understanding of history is helpful also in placing contemporary issues in broader perspective. This too is often lacking in a world structured by neoliberal systems and policies. There is a tendency to deal either just with the here and now, or to become 'future focused' in our thinking. The past can teach, if we know how to 'listen' to it and provided we are not too quick in imposing our present categories of understanding on others from distant generations. A posture of radical openness is needed, where the present, the past and possible futures can be contemplated with care and humility (Freire, 1976, 1998a; Peters & Roberts, 2011). The desire for instant gratification is very much a feature of our current moment in history, and this phenomenon finds its way into education. But Freire was aware that higher education in particular has a key role to play in slowing us down somewhat – in prompting us to pause, to ponder, to think again about what we want and why. When we allow this process to work, we can often find that what at first seemed most obvious, least questionable, is rather more problematic than we imagined. We can sometimes discover that alternatives to our current social and economic arrangements have been sitting in front of us all along, even if only in nascent form. A seemingly simple idea – e.g., favoring cooperation instead of competition – can assume far greater importance than we imagined if we are prepared to consider, fully and fairly, some of its broader implications for policy and practice.

The University and Critical Citizenship Education

Freire expressed his concerns about neoliberalism in the years immediately following the fall of the Berlin Wall and the collapse of the Soviet empire. For some, these momentous events signaled the beginning of a new era, a world order utterly dominated by one mode of production. It was assumed that debate over the best way to organize social and economic life was now over: capitalism has triumphed, and the possibility of a socialist future had disappeared for ever. Freire sounded a warning about the danger of becoming too certain of one's certainties, of becoming smug, unreflective and dismissive of opposing positions (Freire, 1994, 1997b). This, he felt, was one of the defining features of neoliberal thought. Not only that; he saw a kind of fatalism at work in neoliberal discourses: an almost casual acceptance of ongoing social inequalities as inevitable (Freire, 1998a, 2004, 2007). He refused to give in to this kind of thinking and fought hard, right up to his death, to demonstrate the flaws and consequences of this fatalistic mindset.

What would he have made, then, of the years that followed? In his native Brazil, the political party he had supported – the Brazilian Workers Party – went on to win power, with Luiz Inácio Lula da Silva ('Lula') serving as President of the country from 2003 to 2011. The shifts in policy thinking during the first decade of the 21st century, not only in Brazil but also in several other South American countries (e.g., Venezuela, Argentina, and Bolivia), have prompted some commentators to speak of the emergence of a *post*-neoliberal age (Grugel & Riggirozzi, 2012; Lewkowicz, 2015). It is possible to see other changes – e.g., the emergence of 'Third Way' politics in the United Kingdom and elsewhere, and the 'Occupy' movements that followed the global financial crisis – as further indications that the term 'neoliberalism' is no longer helpful in describing contemporary policy trends. Yet, as Springer (2015) observes, it is important not to treat neoliberalism as a 'monolithic, static, and undifferentiated end-state' (p. 5). Neoliberalism is a doctrine with a certain elasticity; it is a way of thinking about human beings and the world that has left its mark in a variety of different ways. We might say, more correctly, that there is no *one* neoliberalism; strictly speaking, what we have observed is a plurality of neoliberalism*s*, each with their own distinctive characteristics in specific contexts, at given times, but all linked to each other by some common trends and ideas.

Some of the features of neoliberalism that troubled Freire most have persisted, or been reasserted, in Brazil and other countries. Policies of renationalization and government efforts to provide further support to the most vulnerable members of society have, in the longer term, proved inadequate in significantly reducing economic inequalities. The culture of relentless consumption is, if anything, growing more pervasive across the globe. Instrumentalist views of knowledge and education have prevailed over other conceptions, and the idea of securing an economic advantage in a competitive world has remained a key policy goal. New forms of privatization in education have emerged. Neoliberalism may have 'imploded' with the banking and mortgage crises of 2007/2008 (Hall, Massey, & Rustin, 2013), but in the second decade of the 21st century it rebounded strongly. In some countries (including New Zealand) the housing market, particularly in bigger cities, has been buoyant, widening existing gaps between 'haves' and 'have-nots.' Clothing, shoes, and other consumer goods continue to be produced via 'sweat shop' labour in massive factories, with appalling wages and conditions for workers, for global markets. The worldwide pandemic of 2020/2021 has thrown up new challenges, but in many countries, the concern has been to return, as quickly as possible, to 'business as usual.' Few in positions of political leadership have been prompted by the Covid-19 crisis to reassess the way 'business' is carried out in contemporary economies. Whether our current age is best described as neoliberal or post-neoliberal, there is, from a Freirean perspective, still considerable work to do.

One way of thinking about this 'work' in institutions such as universities is to conceive of it as a process of critical citizenship education. There is a substantial body of theoretical work on citizenship, globalization, and education.[4] Comparatively little has been said, however, about what we might call 'academic citizenship.'[5] As academics, we live as citizens not just outside the gates of the university but within our institutions. The values we embody in our work with students and colleagues are often the same as those we espouse and exemplify in other spheres of life. How we approach the task of 'being an academic' depends very much on what we understand by citizenship. Many teachers, not just in universities but in institutions at all levels in the education system, are committed to their jobs not just for financial reasons but because they genuinely want to make a worthwhile difference in other lives.[6] But in teaching others, we are not just playing a part in shaping their futures; we are also in forming ourselves as ethical beings. Our service responsibilities – e.g., on committees, within the wider community, and to our discipline – also contribute to this process of formation. If it is *critical* academic citizenship education in particular with which we are concerned here, what might this mean? New Zealand again provides an interesting case study in addressing this question.

While New Zealand has often been seen as one of the 'least impure' examples of neoliberal reform (Jessop, 2002), at least during the period when the core economic changes were being instituted (1984–1990), even in this country, and especially in the social policy domain of tertiary education, neoliberalism has evolved in uneven, messy steps. This 'impurity' is, potentially, a source of some hope for those who work in the tertiary sector. Managerialism continues to exert a dominant influence over university life but this is by no means a complete victory for neoliberalism. New Zealand academics have resisted neoliberal reforms from the beginning. They have done so in a range of different ways, sometimes quietly, sometimes loudly, both via individual actions and in various collectives. The Tertiary Education Union has played a significant role in this process, and sometimes academics have protested on the streets over cuts to funding, the closing of programs of study, and other matters of concern. Some scholars have written critical pieces for daily newspapers, and others have appeared regularly on television to debate contentious educational issues. Equally important are the less visible forms

---

4   See, for example, Haynes (2009), Pashby (2011), Peters, Britton, and Blee (2008), Petrovic and Kuntz (2014), and Veugelers (2011).
5   A related line of inquiry examines the role of the intellectual from a Freirean point of view. A helpful source in exploring that avenue is Torres (1994c).
6   Freire was highly critical of the comparatively low salaries paid to teachers (see Freire, 1997b). His point was not that teachers should be driven by money in their career decisions but that teaching is not given the respect it deserves.

of resistance enacted through teaching and supervision. These may be evident in the questions university teachers ask, the problems they draw to the attention of students, the readings they recommend and make available, the forms of dialogue and reflection they foster, and the implied understanding of the purpose of education they convey, among other ways.

In New Zealand, universities are required under the law to accept a role as 'critic and conscience of society.' There is thus some legal protection for academics who speak out, but there are limits to this – particularly in teaching. Universities can and do impose their own restrictions on curriculum content and academic conduct. For the most part, academics are keenly aware of the sense of responsibility that accompanies the ideal of academic freedom. Cases suggesting an abuse of this freedom are relatively rare. Also unusual, though not unheard of, are examples of direct Ministerial interference in matters relating to an academic's teaching. University classrooms are never entirely open spaces, but even in otherwise quite oppressive managerialist environments, they can still create opportunities for the investigation and exploration of alternative modes of thinking, being, and social organization. Serving as a 'critic of society' in such spaces does not, from a Freirean perspective, mean the principal task of the academic is simply to 'criticize.' Critique is an important form of academic activity but this is ultimately a constructive exercise. Freire's critique of global neoliberal capitalism was simultaneously an expression of his deep commitment to social justice and the ideal of humanization.[7]

The notion of serving as the 'conscience' of society invites further questions. The idea of being a vehicle for, or an expression of, anyone else's conscience is problematic (Roberts, 2007b). A more fruitful way of looking at this, with Freire in mind, is to see *having* a conscience, of one's own, and *exercising* this, as a pedagogical virtue in university environments. Allowing the voice of conscience to work on us as we conduct our daily academic activities is critical if we are to live with integrity in university environments. The formation of academics as critical citizens can be seen as a process of conscientization. This concept is one of the most complex in Freire's philosophy, and it was a frequent source of misunderstanding (as Freire saw it) among his interpreters – so much so that for a time, Freire stopped using the term. Essential to conscientization is the development of a deeper, more critical understanding of the societies in which we live. But just as important, and often forgotten, is the element of 'conscience' in conscientization (Freire, 2004; Liu, 2014). Our consciences provide a bridge between the reflective and active aspects of humanizing praxis. A well-developed conscience allows us to engage in a kind of inner dialogue, and this can be in the midst of an external dialogue with

---

7   Cf. Freire (1993, 1994, 1998a, 2004, 2007), Kirylo (2011), McLaren (2000), Rozas (2007).

others, prompting us to action. Our consciences won't let us go; they keep prodding away at us. The academic citizen who is able to listen, attentively, calmly and with a sense of equanimity, to the insistent voice of his or her conscience, will often have a sharper awareness of what he or she is committed to and why. This does not make academic life any easier; indeed, it will often mean taking the harder, more complex, more stressful, more time-consuming path.

A Freirean approach to critical citizenship education places human beings, not the economy, at the center of any tertiary institution. The humanities have been marginalized under neoliberalism; for an academic committed to Freirean education, they are vital. In particular, Freire would have said, we need to ask and address fundamental ontological, epistemological, ethical, and political questions: 'What does it mean to be a human being? What is the nature of reality? What is 'knowledge' and how do we come to know? What ought we to do? (How should we live? How should we structure our society?) What are the impediments to the realization of our ideals?' (Roberts, 2014, pp. 232–233). Critical citizenship education conceived in these terms recognizes that much of what matters most in education is not, or ought not to be, measurable. The immeasurability, uncertainty, and unpredictability of education need not be abhorred or ignored but can instead be celebrated. A critical academic citizen in the Freirean sense will not be afraid to declare that he or she approaches university life as an act of love. This is not romantic love but love as care, attention, and commitment: love for the students we teach, for the colleagues with whom we work, and for the act of study. Students, Freire would want to say, must not be seen as 'consumers' of education but as active, critical participants in the process of constructing and advancing knowledge. Critical academic citizens will, where appropriate to the course of study, find ways to encourage pedagogical engagement with the most pressing global issues of the day (e.g., climate change and terrorism). Such an approach to critical citizenship education recognizes that there is no *one* best way to teach, or to understand the world, or to live in that world. At the same time, the acknowledgment of a plurality of different views should not stop us from saying that some ways are better than others. Freire would have wanted us to give his way, his philosophy and pedagogy, a fair hearing, but as part of a much wider ongoing intellectual conversation and in relation to the distinctive themes and problems of our time and place.

CHAPTER FOUR

Thesis Supervision

A Freirean Approach

As a teacher, Paulo Freire is best known for his adult literacy work with impoverished urban and rural communities in Brazil in the 1950s and early 1960s. He developed an innovative and highly effective approach to the teaching of reading and writing, enabling adults to attain basic literacy skills in as little as 40 hours. In linking the reading of the word with the reading of the world, Freire provided an opportunity for participants to reflect critically on their circumstances and experiences. The ongoing development of Freire's literacy program was interrupted by the military coup in Brazil in 1964, and Freire was forced into exile. Within a few short years, however, and particularly following the publication of *Pedagogy of the Oppressed* (Freire, 1972a), the principles that had informed his teaching would attract international attention. Freire's emphasis on dialogue, the posing of problems, and the development of critical consciousness in teaching and learning generated much discussion and influenced countless educators in the decades that followed. Freire would go on to deepen and extend many of the key ideas that formed the heart of his early books, his dialogical collaborations with other intellectuals proving particularly fruitful in this process.[1] Near the end of his life, teaching remained a key

---

1   By 'early books,' I mean *Education: The Practice of Freedom* (Freire, 1976), *Pedagogy of the Oppressed* (Freire, 1972a), and *Cultural Action for Freedom* (Freire, 1972b). See also Torres (2014). Freire's 'talking books,' composed in the form of a structured dialogue with others, include Escobar

focus of his work, as is evident from the content of several posthumously published texts.²

One aspect of Freire's work on teaching that is sometimes somewhat neglected is his interest in higher education. Freire held university posts in Brazil following his return to his home country in 1980, and he also took up a number of short-term appointments as an academic visitor in other parts of the world. Among his corpus of published works is one specifically devoted to higher education (Escobar et al., 1994), but there are also references to teaching and learning in university settings in a number of his other books. In *A Pedagogy for Liberation* (Freire & Shor, 1987), for example, Freire considers what, how and why students in higher education should read, and in *Politics and Education* (Freire, 1998c) there is an essay on the tasks of the Catholic university. Freire has much to offer in considering the nature and purpose of the university and, more broadly, the role of the critical intellectual in society (Roberts, 2010; Torres, 1994b). This chapter will concentrate on one specific form of university teaching, namely, thesis supervision (or 'advising' as Freire refers to it).³ There has been comparatively little attention paid to supervision by Freirean commentators. It is true that Freire did not address this topic at length, but there is an important, and seldom mentioned, chapter on the role of thesis and dissertation advisors in *Letters to Cristina* (Freire, 1996), and this will provide the initial focus for discussion here. Freire, it will be argued, offers a distinctive approach to supervision as a transformative teaching and learning process – an orientation that places him at odds with prevailing trends in higher education (cf. Espinoza, 2017). Freire's comments on supervision provide an avenue for elucidating and exploring other pivotal dimensions of his philosophy and pedagogy, and thus warrant closer scrutiny.

Freire on the Role of Thesis Advisors

Freire published his book, *Letters to Cristina: Reflections on My Life and Work*, in 1996. In its careful, systematic development of ideas, and in its blending of pedagogical theory with reflections on personal experience, it is among the best of his later works. It is perhaps the richest account we have of the formative part

---

et al. (1994), Freire and Faundez (1989), Freire and Macedo (1987), Freire and Shor (1987), and Horton and Freire (1990).
2 E.g., Freire (1998a, b, c, 2004, 2007).
3 In this chapter, the terms 'supervisor' and 'advisor' will be used interchangeably. The terms 'student,' 'candidate' and 'advisee' will also be treated as equivalents.

played by Freire's earlier years in the development of his educational theory and practice. The title of the work comes from a request Freire received from his niece, Cristina: 'I would like ... for you to write me letters about your life, your childhood and, little by little, about the trajectory that led you to become the educator you are now' (Freire, 1996, p. 11). Consistent with this request, the book is structured in the form of eighteen letters, each of which takes up a given theme or topic. The sixteenth letter addresses questions relating to thesis supervision. It conveys some clear, practical points of advice for supervisors and thesis students while also inviting deeper reflection on key themes in Freire's educational theory. The letter thus lends itself well to multiple readings. It might be taken up by those who are relatively new to the supervision process and read as a realistic account of what they can or should expect of themselves and the candidates with whom they work. Or, it might serve as a prompt for a wider discussion of the ontological, epistemological and ethical dimensions of educational experience. Or, it could provide an entry point for comparing Freire's approach to teaching and learning with other competing views.

Freire argues that the role of the advisor should not be one of 'programming the candidate's intellectual life or establishing rules about what the latter may or may not write about' (p. 167); instead, the assistance that is provided should enable candidates to help themselves. Candidates need to listen carefully to their supervisors, but the reverse is also true. Supervisors should communicate in an 'open and friendly manner' with students, both supporting them and challenging them (p. 167). The supervisor-student relationship is, Freire maintains, 'more than a strictly intellectual one and must be warm, respectful, and capable of creating a climate of mutual trust rather than curbing the advisee's production' (p. 167). Providing helpful answers to questions and making useful suggestions for reading are important, but these forms of assistance should also encourage the candidate to ask further questions. The 'comfort' furnished by the attitude of the supervisor toward the student should not be *too* comfortable; students must also feel slightly restless. This, as Freire sees it, is a fundamental part of the process of learning through life: 'Quietude cannot be a permanent state. Only within a relationship that is agitated can quietude make sense. Life is a constant search that cannot, even when writing theses and dissertations, be immobilized' (p. 167).

The advisor's role, Freire counsels, is 'to discuss – as many times as may be necessary within the limits of the advisor's time – the development of the advisee's research and ideas; the depth of the advisee's language; the difficulties the advisee faces with the topic, the bibliography, or the very act of reading and studying; and the loyalty with which the advisee writes about topics or people' (pp. 167–168). Supervisors can, Freire notes, also point candidates to lesser known sources and assist them in meeting other intellectuals in their field of study. Advisors have a right – indeed, a duty – to explain how and why they disagree with candidates when points of difference arise, but they do not have a right to *impose* their views on those with whom they work (p. 168). In keeping with his wider educational theory, Freire argues against both authoritarianism (the imposing of one's will on another, with the intent to impede questioning and debate) and permissiveness (where an 'anything goes' attitude prevails). Good supervisors undertake their work with humility, recognizing that they both teach and learn from the students with whom they work (p. 169). They motivate and inspire thesis candidates, enabling them to draw the best from themselves. But this takes effort and commitment on the part of the candidate, and where this is lacking, the supervisor also has a responsibility to comment on this (p. 168). The seriousness of the task must be emphasized; work on a doctoral or Master's thesis is a major undertaking, requiring long hours, concentration, and persistence in the face of difficulties.

Freire encourages those completing theses to engage regularly and extensively in both reading and writing (p. 169). These activities stimulate and inform each other. Forming the habit of writing daily, even if it is not always on a topic directly relevant to the thesis, is important. Similarly, if a scholar is to write well, reading widely and well is crucial. Freire values clarity and elegance in written expression; there is, he says, 'no conflict between writing with rigour and writing beautifully' (p. 170). Beauty can be found not just in the world of art but in academic work, and those who engage in the latter can gain a great deal from reading not just the canonical texts in their field but also the writings of novelists, poets, and biographers (p. 170). There should, in Freire's view, be little difference between a good book and a good thesis; both, it might be said, should have a certain aesthetic appeal, each in a manner appropriate to the task at hand. Freire acknowledges that writing is not easy, but if we are prepared to put in sufficient effort, over a sustained period of time, it is possible to experience genuine joy through the act of writing (p. 172).

Having opportunities to share thesis ideas with others, including both other students and other advisors, can also be of great value in sharpening one's thinking, improving one's writing, and better understanding what one is reading. Freire recalls a process he established with a colleague at the Pontifical Catholic University of São Paulo that involved meeting with graduate students to discuss their theses. The meetings were three hours long, with a brief break for coffee, and involved several related steps. Students would first speak about how they came into the program of study and would comment on their evolving topic areas. These verbal reports would then be debated, with questions and suggestions from others. Freire suggests that discussing one's work in this way contributes directly to the writing of the thesis: 'Talking about what one intends to write and what one has already written about helps one to better write what one has not written and rewrite what has not been finished' (p. 171). The process Freire and his colleague instituted had other benefits as well. It fostered curiosity among participants in the discussions, and it allowed students to see things in their work that hadn't been visible without the feedback provided by others. These encounters encouraged candidates to consider new perspectives and to build on their existing views. Even where key ideas were retained, the reasons for doing so could become clearer (pp. 171–172).

The supervisor's role is not limited to providing academic advice; there is also a strong element of pastoral care built into the process, when examined from a Freirean perspective. Good supervisors come to care deeply for the students with whom they work. Occasionally, the relationship between a supervisor and a student may become strained. Compatibility between supervisors and candidates is vital, and when this breaks down, action to address the situation must be taken. Freire is adamant that both parties should have the right, at any time, to choose to discontinue their working relationship (p. 168). Supervision is demanding for both the advisor and the advisee. Advisees must be realistic about what they know and do not know (p. 172), and sometimes they are unable to see this without the guidance of a good supervisor. Equally, it might be inferred from Freire's comments, supervisors are not always able to see some of their own weaknesses until they begin the process of working with a student. In the end, both the supervisor and the candidate need to recognize and value the ethical character of the relationship into which they enter, acknowledging each other's humanity. The advisee, like the advisor, is a being who 'feels, suffers, dreams, knows, and can know more' (p. 172). For the supervision process to work well, for both supervisors and students, dedication and commitment must be combined with courtesy, respect, and a willingness to listen and learn.

Supervision in Contemporary University Environments

Freire's advice to supervisors and students relies upon a construct of the human being that is, in many respects, out of kilter with the spirit of our times. In most countries of the Western world, for more than three decades, the ideology of neoliberalism, in all its permutations, has played a dominant role in structuring economic and social change (Flew, 2014; Harvey, 2005; Torres, 2009). As noted in the previous chapter, neoliberals construe human beings as essentially self-centered, self-interested individual choosers and consumers. When applied in university contexts, this way of thinking suggests that decisions about what and how to study will be made principally on economic grounds. Students will seek to secure an advantage for themselves in competing for jobs and salaries in a competitive world. They will in most cases want to complete their studies as quickly and as effortlessly as possible. Their relationship with a supervisor is based on a business model: the student pays fees to the university and expects services to be provided in return for this investment.

The institutional expression of neoliberal ideas in the university can be seen in the philosophy and practices of managerialism. There is an emphasis on performance, efficiency, and revenue generation, with clear, hierarchical divisions between 'management' and other academics in the university. Institutions compete vigorously with each other for students, reputational advancement, and sources of income. Knowledge is viewed as a commodity; as something to be traded, with 'sellers' and 'buyers.' The buyers can include students (local, national, and international), the government, policy bodies, foundations, or corporations. Large sums of money are devoted to marketing in order to create distinctive institutional brands. Supervisors are important in this model to the extent that they allow the institution to meet its 'key performance indicators' (KPIs), and they are expected to minimize the wastage of time in their efforts. They are encouraged to take on top students who will create few 'complications' and finish on time. Full-time candidates are strongly preferred over part-timers. 'Performance' is measured and monitored via a bureaucratic process that involves the filling in of forms, the calculation of workloads (often based largely on student numbers and/or dollars generated), and completion rates. Full fee-paying international students, often sponsored by their governments or employers, are favored, provided such candidates do not end up creating other demands on time and resources (e.g., in developing the required abilities in the language of instruction).

In some contexts, thesis students become sources of revenue in other ways. They generate funds for institutions not just in the fees they pay (and in any government subsidy that accompanies these fees) but also in performance-based research funding schemes. New Zealand's performance-based research fund (PBRF), for example, provides the main mechanism for distributing government funds for research in universities and other tertiary education organizations (see further, Roberts, 2013). Funding is determined on the basis of performance in three areas. First, individual academics are required to submit 'Evidence Portfolios' (EPs) and these are evaluated by panels of their peers. Second, institutions and organizations are rewarded for the amount of external research income they generate. The third element of the funding framework is research degree completions. This third component is the one that is most obviously linked with the work of thesis students and their supervisors, but not exclusively so. In medicine, engineering and the sciences, research is often conducted in teams, with projects that are sustained by significant external funding. Thesis students may be 'attached' to these projects, and their topics may even be determined for them by other more senior researchers in the project team. In the EPs completed by individual academics too, thesis students may play a role in boosting ratings and income. Academics are sometimes strongly encouraged to demand the right to be listed as co-authors on any thesis-related publications completed by the students they supervise. This practice increases the number of research 'outputs' in an academic's EP and, other things being equal, gives it a better chance of achieving a higher rating.

Freire regarded neoliberal ideas, policies, and practices as deeply problematic.[4] The ontology underpinning Freirean pedagogy, including the process of supervision, differs markedly from the concept of the individual that lies at the heart of neoliberalism. For Freire, while we may sometimes be driven self-interest, this need not always be the case; we can, and do, seek to serve the interests of others rather than simply satisfying our own wants. Supervision is a prime example of a relationship structured by an ethos of service to others. The supervisor needs to be humble, committed, caring, and attentive. *Love* is a key element of the supervision process, as it is for Freirean education more generally (Darder, 2002; Fraser, 1997; Roberts, 2010). Freire, as we have seen in previous chapters, speaks of love for the students with whom teachers work, as well as love for both the object and task of studying. For supervisors, the focus is on doing everything that is necessary, within the constraints of a given institutional environment, to enable the student to flourish, both intellectually and as an ethical human being. This entails careful observation of changes in the student's demeanor, study habits, written work, and verbal contributions to thesis discussions. Subtle shifts can be important. Often the significance of a remark or a gesture or a sentence will only become clear following several days of reflection. The work of a thesis supervisor, in this sense, never goes away; it continues beyond the hours for which the supervisor is paid and it cannot be neatly contained within rigid workload models. Supervision requires a form of sacrifice on the part of the supervisor, not just in terms of placing the needs of the student ahead of his or her own career advancement, but also in the emotional energy that must be committed to the process. Freire (1985) stresses the demanding nature of study but he would also be quick to admit that supervision can be physically, mentally, and emotionally exhausting. Supervisors must walk a fine line between giving too much and giving too little. They want to assist students in every way possible, through all the highs and lows associated with the

---

4   See Freire (1994, 1997a, 1998a, 2004, 2007).

writing of a thesis, but must also stay sufficiently healthy to be able to continue to provide such assistance in the future.

Under managerialism, the relationship between a supervisor and a student is regarded as a form of contract; for Freire, it is much more complicated than that. Through supervision, both students and their supervisors can learn to better appreciate the connectedness between different elements of educational experience. From a Freirean point of view, we can only understand ourselves adequately as individuals when see ourselves as part of a wider context, where the roles played by others are pivotal in shaping our thoughts, feelings, and actions. We are social beings rather than isolated individuals, conditioned (though never fully determined: Freire, 1997a) by the circumstances in which we live, work and communicate. Neoliberalism has played a dominant role in shaping tastes, wants, and patterns of consumption, but one of the aims of education at the Master's or doctoral level should be to encourage the interrogation of everyday experience. Freire was concerned with the formation of *critical* subjects, not merely *consuming* subjects. He wanted students, and their supervisors, to seek to *know* and not merely to *perform*. Supervision is a profoundly important intervention in the life of another person; when the relationship works as Freire believes it should, neither the supervisor nor the student will ever be quite the same again. Often students will stay in touch with their supervisors for years or decades after their theses have been completed. But even where this is not the case, the influence of the supervisor on the life of the student will continue to be felt, in the way the student approaches problems, deals with ethical dilemmas, and relates to others.

If the primary motivation of the supervisor is to help the student, advice and guidance in publishing from the thesis can be given freely and fully with no expectation of co-authorship. Freire's position, it will be recalled, is that advisors should be trying to help advisees to help themselves. Supervisors can assist students by reading and reviewing their draft papers, suggesting possible journals, and helping them to understand and negotiate the rigors of peer review. They can draw on their knowledge, experience, and standing with peers in supporting and guiding candidates as they seek to present their work at conferences and publish their thesis work in book form. They can advise on the preparation of proposals and recommend the student's work to colleagues who serve as series editors for international academic book publishers. These forms of assistance can be seen as part of the ethical commitment the advisor makes to the advisee in taking on the task of supervision. The 'reward' for the supervisor is the sense of quiet satisfaction that comes from seeing the student succeed, not just in his or her publishing endeavors but also in his or her development as a scholar and as a person. A supervisor committed to Freirean principles will want to value and promote the intellectual independence and integrity of the student, and the guidance provided after a thesis has been completed will often be as important in reinforcing this goal as the advice given during the period of enrollment.

Underpinning Freire's advice to supervisors and students is his ideal of humanization. Freirean humanization, as has been argued earlier, is a process of praxical transformation: a critical, dialogical synthesis of reflection and action (Freire, 1972a). The task of completing a thesis, in the manner described by Freire in *Letters to Cristina*, has the potential to be transformative in exactly this way. Freire did not intend humanization to be conceived in linear or mechanical terms. Humanization is a dynamic, often unpredictable, always changing, moment by moment process. Its constituent elements are not 'steps' to be taken in a fixed order, or requirements that can be 'ticked off' in a kind of performance review. The connections between reflection and action are much more dynamic and fluid than that. The defining features of humanization may be universal (Freire, 1998a) but these key elements manifest themselves in distinct ways in different contexts. Good supervisors encourage students to reflect deeply at all stages in their thesis journey, whether this is in conceiving of a problem and developing research questions, reviewing the literature, gathering data, or developing an argument. But this reflection must be intertwined with the active disciplines of writing and speaking. Both the reflective and the active elements of humanization are evident in the critical, purposeful dialogue Freire sees as essential to education. Dialogue for Freire is not aimless, casual conversation; rather, it has a sense of structure and direction (Freire & Shor, 1987; Roberts, 2000). In a supervision relationship, then, moments for dialogue – whether in formally scheduled meetings, or in e-mail exchanges, or at conferences, or in informal discussions – must be regarded as of the utmost importance for the overall progress of the thesis project.

The need for structure, rigor, and direction in Freirean dialogue does not mean thesis conversations have to adhere to rigid rules or procedures; nor should they become formulaic or predictable. Among the virtues Freire espoused was openness, and this has particular relevance in the realm of supervision. One of Freire's principal objections to neoliberalism was its excessive certainties (Roberts, 2010). Neoliberals may look favorably on the idea of open markets but there is, Freire felt, also a profound sense of closure in neoliberal discourses (cf. Toh, 2017). There is a certainty that neoliberal global capitalism is the only legitimate mode of production – the only reasonable form of social and economic organization – and that any talk of alternatives is not to be taken seriously. Freire, as we have seen, was open in declaring his support for democratic socialism, but was aware that reference to socialist ideals would be dismissed as old-fashioned, utopian (in a pejorative sense), and unhelpful in our current age.[5] As Freire saw it, neoliberalism was characterized by a certain smugness and fatalism. Neoliberals lacked both an appreciation for history and a willingness to question the ideas implicit in their ways of thinking and acting. Such attitudes, he argued, have no place in education. In completing a thesis, openness is necessary if a spirit of investigation is to be brought to life. Dialogue between supervisors and students can play a vital role in nurturing this approach to inquiry. Openness, like freedom, is always exercised within limits – some of which are generated by supervisors and students themselves, others of which are externally imposed.

A supervision meeting may have an 'agenda' (imparting a sense of structure and purpose), but neither the supervisor nor the student can know quite where their discussion will take them. There must be sufficient freedom within a dialogical situation for surprises to arise, with differing viewpoints being given adequate space to interact with each other. There is no 'perfect' or 'pure' space for dialogue, and the forms of authority that structure a thesis discussion must be acknowledged and considered (cf. Freire & Shor, 1987). Students and supervisors must share enough in common to be able to communicate, to empathize, and to understand (in some fashion) but it is their differences that provide the motor for dialogue (cf. Freire, 1997a, b; Freire & Macedo, 1993, 1995; Roberts, 2000; Rosaz Gomez, 2007). The same point applies to the works the student reads and reflects upon in completing a thesis. Without some critical points of difference, there is no basis for an active, productive 'conversation' with other authors, past and present; nor can the student make the original contribution to knowledge that is expected for a doctoral thesis. For Freire, uncertainty, while sometimes debilitating, can also be a source of hope, and this can sustain rather than impede a student who is genuinely open to allowing the process of investigation to do its work in forming him or her as a scholar. Thus, while Freire stresses the need for preparation and planning on the part of the student (and the supervisor), this is not in order to close off the possibility of a thesis dialogue developing in a new, unanticipated direction; rather, this prior work is necessary if both the student and the supervisor are to be ready to make the most of such moments when they arise.

In contemporary universities, pressure is frequently exerted to get students through their studies as quickly and painlessly as possible. Freire understood that part of the value of studying seriously, and of supervising students who are doing so, lies in the difficulties posed by thesis work. Completing a thesis, Freire would have said, is not *meant* to be easy; it should demand something extraordinary of

---

5 Cf. Farrell, Angel, and Vahl (2017), Freire (1998a, 2004, 2007), Liu (2014), Roberts and Freeman-Moir (2013).

both the student and the supervisor. Pain and suffering are thus not necessarily to be avoided at all costs; they may have something worthwhile to contribute to the learning process and to the quality of the scholarship (cf. Chen, 2011, 2016; Roberts, 2016). Struggling with an idea, wrestling with it, can be a process that takes hours, days, weeks, or even *years*, but despite the discomfort created by this process, it can sometimes prove to be crucial in seeing a thesis through to completion. It is not at all uncommon for a student to experience a 'breakthrough' in thinking near the very end of his or her studies, realizing at last what he or she had been grappling with, had been trying to say, all along. What is not always recognized when such moments occur is that they have only become possible because of countless smaller moments of persistent, patient, seemingly fruitless effort. The supervisor cannot simply 'plant' the ideas into the student and expect him or her to emerge with the same sense of clarity, understanding, and fulfillment that emerges from long hours of disciplined, but open-minded, reading, writing, and dialogue.

Freire's ideas on advising form but a small part of his overall educational philosophy. It is important not to forget where Freire came from, the challenges he had to face as a teacher and social activist, and the situations of oppression with which he was dealing. Freire's overt linking of education with politics is one of the distinguishing features of his pedagogy.[6] Supervising a thesis in the comfort of a university office might seem to be a world away from the streets of a Brazilian *favela*. Freire's work must be read holistically and it must be contextualized. For Freire, however, there was no intellectual or political divide between his adult literacy work and his advice for supervisors and thesis students. For Freire, the realm of 'politics' isn't confined to the actions of politicians, or to social movements that seek to overthrow oppressive regimes, or to struggles between groups with opposing views on the economy or the environment. It is present in everything we do as educationists (Freire & Shor, 1987; Roberts, 2010; Shor, 1993). The political nature of a supervision process will be evident in how supervisors and students understand themselves as human beings, how they interact with each other, and what they hope to gain from the process. It is there in the smallest moments of discussion, investigation, joy, and despair. Both students and supervisors feel the weight of institutional politics in the bureaucratic demands placed upon them and in the implicit messages they receive about the comparative value of different forms of knowledge.

---

6 See further, Kirylo (2011), Mayo (1999, 2004), McLaren (1999), Morrow and Torres (2002), Roberts (2000), Rossatto (2005), Schugurensky (2011), and Torres (1993, 1998).

Supervision agreements and university rules now frequently have clauses about 'intellectual property,' reinforcing the view that knowledge is a commodity subject to the same laws that govern commerce outside the walls of the academy. The idea that a university can 'own' the knowledge created through a thesis investigation would, as signaled in the previous chapter, have been repugnant to Freire. In marketized, managerial university environments, there is an increasing separation of 'knowers' from 'knowledge,' as if the latter can exist without the former. 'Knowledge' ends up being reduced to nothing more than information or skills. In this form, it is can be more readily quantified, measured and sold. The value of knowledge becomes nothing more than the *price* of knowledge – whether this is the cost of enrolling in a doctoral degree, or of supporting the students who do so, or of buying and selling what is produced through the thesis process. Freire's work makes is plain that it is the *im*measurable benefits of knowledge and knowing that are often of most value. Completing a thesis not only creates new knowledge; it also creates new knowers. 'Knowing' for Freire is not merely a matter of comprehending or transmitting or trading information. It is not a 'method' (cf. Macedo, 1997; Roberts, 2000). It is a mode of being. Seeking to know through the in-depth investigative work of a thesis transforms our view of ourselves as knowers. This effect can be experienced and observed but to attempt to quantify it, or to measure it or sell it, is to *de*value the knowledge created and dehumanize the knowers involved in this creative act.

Freire's approach to thesis supervision suggests a necessary, and potentially liberating, tension between creativity and discipline. Neither thesis supervisors nor the students with whom they work should be too tightly wedded to traditional forms of scholarly inquiry and research. One of the essential tasks of the university is to challenge accepted wisdom and to foster what we might refer to as intellectual bravery. It takes courage to push against received views, and a thesis, especially at the doctoral level, provides an opportunity to forge new ground, theoretically, methodologically, educationally, and politically. Undertaking serious study is always a *risky* process.[7] In some cases, where the ideas being developed provide a direct and demonstrable challenge or threat to those who occupy powerful positions in a society, the risks may even be life-threatening. But even where the risks are not of this kind, ethical and existential dilemmas and difficulties must be negotiated. As students probe ever more deeply, think ever more critically about themselves and the world, they open themselves up to the possibility of new forms of life where what had hitherto been enjoyed or loathed or ignored may have to be renegotiated. Creativity and courage can also be fostered in the way material is presented in a

---

7   Education can be conceived as a 'beautiful' risk (see Biesta, 2014).

thesis or defended in an examination. But in these contexts, as in other educational situations, discipline is also necessary. Discipline needs to come from both the supervisor and the student. Discipline is needed in moderating passion with reason, in completing tasks despite myriad other demands, and in realizing that the desire to say and do something 'new' also requires a respectful acknowledgment of what has gone before.

Conclusion

Freire's sixteenth chapter in his *Letters to Cristina* is deceptively simple in its structure, style, and substance. On the surface, it might appear as if Freire is merely offering straightforward practical advice, with little reference to matters of theory or politics. It might be claimed that while there are some valuable 'tips' in the letter for new supervisors and their students, those already familiar with the process of supervision will learn nothing new. Such a response would arguably fail to heed the advice that is apparently so well known. The clean, concise, uncluttered prose adopted in the piece is itself an illustration of exemplary writing, and in that sense can teach those who read it. And even if much of the guidance Freire provides is accepted implicitly by experienced academics, this knowledge is not always articulated explicitly; nor is it always organized so coherently and cohesively. In the academic world, it is easy to mistake obscurantism, ambiguity, and confusion for sophistication and depth in understanding, and to be too quickly dismissive of work that seems to 'state the obvious.' Freire is an example of an intellectual who strived to convey ideas in a manner that was simple but not simplistic. Working to reach this standard in written communication is a worthy goal for all academics, whatever their level or experience in the university system.

If time is taken to meditate carefully on Freire's letter, it becomes evident that behind it stands a complex ontological, epistemological, and ethical framework. Supervision can form part of the wider process of humanization, for both advisors and advisees. It can play an important role in allowing both supervisors and students to develop a deeper, more critical understanding of themselves and the social world in which they live. Thesis work can push the boundaries of knowledge and encourage a closer examination of what had previously been taken for granted. Supervision never exists in a vacuum; it always takes place in a context shaped by dominant structures, policies, and ideas. At the time at which Freire was composing his letters to Cristina, neoliberalism provided the dominant policy narrative, and its influence was already being felt in universities. In the succeeding decades, this influence has, if anything, become even more marked. Younger academics and thesis students in many contexts will never have experienced anything else: the logic and languages of marketization and competition, accountability and performance, measurement and management, are the only forms of institutional life they have known. Freire's approach to supervision provides a clear alternative to this way of thinking about the nature and purpose of university life. That such an alternative exists is grounds for ongoing investigation, dialogue, and hope.

CHAPTER FIVE

Knowledge, Culture, and Education

Freire and Dilemmas of Difference

This chapter reflects on an essay review, by Frank Margonis, of one of my earlier books on Freire, *Education, Literacy, and Humanization: Exploring the Work of Paulo Freire* (Roberts, 2000). Many of the key questions and issues raised in this exchange remain relevant to debates over Freire's work today. This is a complicated, ongoing conversation, and I am grateful to Margonis for prompting me to reflect on the epistemological and ethical underpinnings to the argument advanced in *Education, Literacy, and Humanization*. Margonis's thoughtful reading is very much in keeping with the spirit of respectful engagement encouraged by the subject of the book, Paulo Freire. As Freire noted several times in the last years of his life, scholars and activists on the Left have sometimes shown a greater propensity than those on the Right to attack each other in a destructive and divisive manner (see, for example, Freire, 1997a, p. 76). Talk of a shared commitment to dialogue, debate, and the goal of building of a better social world has often been dismissed as 'old hat' – perhaps naïve, perhaps Eurocentric or universalist – and communication between scholars has either disappeared altogether or lapsed into a form of academic nastiness and theoretical infighting. In his essay, Margonis demonstrates a willingness to continue the sort of constructive critical conversation Freire (and many other Left pedagogues) advocated. He sees a certain hope in the Freirean approach to radical education; yet, he also highlights a number of important tensions, problems, and omissions in Freire's work. In this chapter I address some of the issues Margonis raises, while nonetheless accepting that it will not be possible to provide detailed answers to all questions.

An Essentialist Epistemology?

Margonis (2003) concentrates on what might in broad terms be called dilemmas of difference. He addresses the challenges made by theorists such as Bowers (1983) and Ellsworth (1989) to fundamental tenets of Freirean thought, drawing attention to differences between Freire's ethical and pedagogical stance and the worldviews of cultural groups such as the Chipewyan of Canada. Margonis gives both Freire and his critics (and the author) a fair, balanced hearing, and bases his perceptive analysis on a rethinking of Freire's epistemological heritage. He notes that in *Education, Literacy, and Humanization* I drew a contrast between Freire and Plato with respect to the nature of knowledge and the process of knowing. Margonis wants to know 'whether Freire is complicit in the colonial traits of Plato's work' (p. 147). A comparison between the two thinkers is (potentially) critical, Margonis notes, 'if we take Plato to be one of the founders of western thought, and if we also believe that Plato articulated a position that was most conducive to European imperialism' (p. 147). Margonis accepts that Freire may be distinguished from Plato by, among other things, his anti-authoritarianism and his emphasis on the social and historical construction of truth. At the same time, however, Margonis wonders whether 'resonances' of Plato's epistemology remain in Freirean thought. Freire depicts a world which 'can be explained by reference to reasons which describe essences.' This view, Margonis says, 'seems partly descendent from Plato and – more recently – from enlightenment rationalism' (p. 148).

I agree with Margonis that these influences can be detected in Freire's work, and I believe it might have been helpful for me to have clarified my position a little more in the book. Freire's stance on knowledge is 'precisely the opposite' of Plato's in some respects only. While *Education, Literacy, and Humanization* highlights the differences between the two thinkers, there is little explicit discussion of their similarities. As I see it, there are two key issues to be addressed in the light of Margonis's comments. First, we need to ask: To what extent, and in what ways, might Freire's epistemology might be regarded as 'essentialist' and/or 'rationalist'? Second, we need to consider whether Freire's essentialism or rationalism commits him to a form of intervention we cannot defend (as would be the case if it were to be regarded as imperialist or colonialist). My concern here, then, is not merely to ask 'How do Plato and Freire differ in their respective approaches to epistemology?' but also to consider why these differences might *matter*. Margonis's analysis helps us to see that such differences matter a great deal when we consider their ethical and educational implications.

There is an apparent tension between a form of 'constructivism' and a certain kind of 'essentialism' in Freire's epistemology. Freire wants to say that we construct a view of the world, and of ourselves, through social practice – through our interaction with the world (and with others). Knowledge is not 'recollected' (as Plato would have it), or 'bequeathed,' or even – strictly speaking – 'acquired.' Rather, from a Freirean point of view, we *create* knowledge through critical, dialogical reflection and action. At the same time, however, as I point out in the book, Freire is not what might be called an epistemological relativist. For Freire, some ways of attempting to know the world are better than others. Freire highlights a number of dispositions characteristic of those seeking to know: such seekers should, he says, adopt a curious, probing, searching, humble, open-minded attitude toward the world. These qualities are important, Freire believes, if we are to develop a genuinely critical approach toward the object of our investigation. In the book, I chose my words carefully. In discussing Freire's conception of the process of knowing, I stated:

> Given that all aspects of reality exist in a constant state of change, it follows that we can never know absolutely: we can, at best, come closer to knowing the 'raison d'être which explains the object [of study]'. Knowing involves searching for the reason for (or behind) the existence of an object or fact. (Roberts, 2000, pp. 37–38)

It is not difficult to see how a connection with Plato might be drawn. Freire seems to imply that when we seek to know, we are searching for something that might be described as the 'essence' of our object of investigation. Freire's references over the years to searching for the deeper meaning or deeper significance of an object or process or event seem to lend further weight to the view that his epistemology is essentialist. Freire advocates a form of 'epistemological encircling,' where we work our way around an object, attempting to establish deeper and deeper layers of meaning in our understanding of it. Note, however, that in each case we are speaking of searching for something – not of finding it. We cannot find it, according to Freire, because the object of our investigation never 'stands still.' We can never quite 'pin it down': the object is, as Freire puts it, not yet because it is becoming (Freire & Shor, 1987, p. 82). For Freire, then, what we are searching for when we seek to know is not Platonic Forms – the unchanging Ideas behind transitory and imperfect physical appearances – but rather the ever-changing reality of this world. It is the process of seeking or searching that is the key to Freire's epistemology. Freire's position is that we can (and ought to) seek to find the essence of something, but in doing so we must realize that in the process of seeking to know, the object of our investigation keeps changing.

I turn now to the question of Freire's 'rationalism.' Margonis is correct, I believe, in noting that Freire is indebted to Plato and philosophers of the enlightenment who emphasize the importance of human reason in understanding and explaining the world. Freire's portrait of critical consciousness in his early work is compatible in a number of important respects with the rationalist ideals espoused by liberal thinkers in Education and other fields. Critical consciousness, Freire says in *Education: The Practice of Freedom*, is characterized by:

> ..... depth in the interpretation of problems; by the substitution of causal principles for magical explanations; by the testing of one's 'findings' and by openness to revision; by the attempt to avoid distortion when perceiving problems and to avoid preconceived notions when analyzing them; by refusing to transfer responsibility; by rejecting passive positions; by soundness of argumentation. (Freire, 1976, p. 18)

Yet, there are, even in this, the most 'liberal' of Freire's books, some significant differences in focus and emphasis between Freire and many other thinkers. Freire stresses the need for dialogue, political action, and 'radicalization' (p. 10). With the publication of his landmark text, *Pedagogy of the Oppressed* (Freire, 1972a), Freire's thinking moved further to the Left and even greater stress was placed on the need for collective struggle and revolutionary change. Freire continued to value rational dispositions in later books, and often alluded to the need for clarity in thought, depth in analysis and critique, and an inquiring state of mind as indispensable features of intellectual and educational life. In many senses, then, he might be said to draw heavily on 'rationalist' traditions from Plato onwards. His faith in the power of human reasoning has, however, always been coupled with a commitment to a wider set of ethical and political goals. The Freirean ideal of critical consciousness is concerned with political change, not merely with a change in thinking.[1] Freire's focus on social structures and political action distinguishes him not just from liberal philosophers and educationists who advance the ideal of rational autonomy but also from many who count themselves as members of the 'critical thinking' movement. Reason, from a Freirean point of view, can take many forms and need not become simply another means, as Ellsworth (1989) might claim, for reinforcing and perpetuating structures and relations of oppression. Freire's work suggests that reason does not belong exclusively to any culture or social group; it is, as Aristotle argued, a (distinctive) quality or capacity all humans share. Freire can certainly be criticized for his anthropocentric portrayal of differences between

---

1 See further, Cruz (2013), McKeown, Edgar, Spandler, and Carey (2018), Roberts (2000, 2010).

humans and animals, but his concept of human reasoning is, I think, considerably more expansive than that furnished by many other 'rationalists.'

Reason and Emotion Revisited

At the same time, it must be acknowledged that Freire could have said more about human qualities other than reason. The nature and role of emotions, in particular, was by no means unimportant to him, but his exploration of the significance of them for education – and indeed for human life more broadly – was somewhat limited. Several decades ago, Ann Sherman (1980) drew our attention to an important tension in Freire's early work:

> On the one hand, Freire states that we need certain emotions (e.g., love, mutual trust) in order for dialogue, and thus education for critical consciousness, to develop. These certain emotions are portrayed as essential to the critical, rational process of education for critical consciousness. On the other hand, Freire talks about the necessity of overcoming the emotionality which he sees as one of the prime characteristics of a naive and irrational consciousness. Freire seems to both advocate and decry the role of emotions in developing critical consciousness. (p. 35)

The original context for Freire's discussion of emotion and reason was, as Sherman points out, Brazilian society in transition during the 20th century. Freire believed that if Brazilians were to move from 'closed' to more 'open' forms of social organization, they needed to avoid creating an emotional and irrational climate of change. Emotional behavior, he thought, would lead to adaptation rather than critical participation in the process of democratic change. Sherman also identifies a problematic account of emotion in Freire's analysis of communication. Freire warns against the dangers of emotive individuals influencing others in a group and thereby compromising the critical character of the communicative process. Emotions in this context become analogous, in Sherman's words, to 'diseases.' Freire also sets up an unhelpful dichotomy between emotion and causal understanding. Sherman notes that emotions play an important role for Freire in motivating literacy students to learn (via codifications and words drawn from everyday life), but they are also seen as insufficient for the critical understanding of causality necessary to social reality. In *Pedagogy of the Oppressed* (Freire, 1972a), Freire discusses the significance of qualities such as love, faith, trust, and hope for educative dialogue. Sherman maintains, however, that these notions remain vague and underdeveloped in Freire's work. She argues that Freire gives us 'no insight into how we are to go about developing these emotions or of what they consist' (Sherman, 1980, p. 38). She explains Freire's failure to provide the necessary detail in this way:

> The fact that Freire does not provide us with this information is partially explainable in terms of his previous adherence to a view of emotions as irrational or acritical forces. That is, if Freire has a lingering conception of emotions as totally acritical forces it would not make much sense to discuss critical methods for developing them. Since the methods of development are part of what the end product is, to advocate critical methods for developing emotions would entail that emotions were, at least in part, critical. If Freire believes that emotions are not critical in any way, then it would be somewhat contradictory to discuss critical methods for developing them. (p. 38)

Sherman concludes with an agenda for further research. What is needed, she says, is a new view of emotions 'which can aid us in making the emotion criteria for dialogue meaningful and substantial' (p. 38).

Sherman's work raised some important questions, some of which found at least partial answers in Freire's later publications. Freire's position on the relationship between reason and emotion arguably shifted across his writing career, though this was more a change in emphasis than a radical revision of earlier ideas. Kerry Burch (1999) speaks of Freire's commitment to the development of democratic dispositions. These include 'a passionate engagement with the world' and an 'intense indignation at the perception of social injustice' (p. 127). This is, in part, what distinguishes Freire from liberals (and rationalists) who devalue passion in education and politics. This devaluing is, to use Burch's eloquent phrase, the 'archilles heel of [the liberals'] putative democratic commitment' (p. 127). As Freire continued to reflect on his earlier ideas, and to gain further educational experience in a number of countries, he spoke on many occasions about the importance of love, hope, and other emotions to his ethical and educational ideal. He construed love as a revolutionary virtue. He talked of the need to love the students with whom one worked and, more broadly, of promoting – in part, through critical education – a loving attitude toward humankind. He made it clear that education involves a profound form of commitment to others, and to knowledge, and ultimately to the building of a better social world. This kind of commitment, he believed, was part of what we might call 'love.' Hope became one of the defining themes of his published work in the last decade of his life, and indeed was incorporated in the title of one of his books: *Pedagogy of Hope* (Freire, 1994; see also Macedo, 2013). As I try to show in *Education, Literacy, and Humanization*, Freire never abandoned his ideals, despite the terrible conditions (of poverty, homelessness, malnutrition, exploitation, and discrimination) he observed all around him in Brazil and across the globe. Indeed, his work makes it clear that it is perhaps particularly under such circumstances that hope becomes essential.

In an especially revealing passage in one of his last books, *Pedagogy of Freedom* (Freire, 1998a), Freire captures the importance of connecting in an emotional way with the students he teaches:

> What is to be thought and hoped of me as a teacher if I am not steeped in that other type of knowing that requires that I be open to caring for the well-being of my students and of the educative experience in which I participate? This openness to caring for the well-being of the students does not mean of course that, as a teacher, I am obliged to care for all my students in the same way. What it does mean is that I am not afraid of my feelings and that I know how to express myself effectively in an appropriate and affirming way. It also means that I know how to fulfill authentically my commitment to my students in the context of a specifically human mode of action. In truth, I feel it is necessary to overcome the false separation between serious teaching and the expression of feeling. ... Affectivity is not necessarily an enemy of knowledge or of the process of knowing. (p. 125)

In the last twenty years of his life, Freire frequently spoke of the joy of writing, his love and passion for reading, and the beauty of books.[2] During this period, he moved to a position in which emotion and reason became tightly integrated with each other. He tried to cultivate a rich life of feeling as a part of his concept of a truly critical approach to teaching, reading, writing, and studying. Emotion was not merely compatible with his critical ideal, but a condition of its very existence. A critical stance, for Freire, became one in which a person would be involved with his or her whole being – physical, emotional, intellectual, and spiritual – in a purposeful activity. Teaching is one example of such an activity, but there are many other fields of human endeavor in which the same qualities of love, hope, care, passion, commitment, and rigor might become essential. Freire's position is beautifully captured in these words, published posthumously in *Teachers as Cultural Workers*:

> [T]he task of the teacher, who is also a learner, is both joyful and rigorous. It demands seriousness and scientific, physical, emotional, and affective preparation. It is a task that requires that those who commit themselves to teaching develop a certain love not only of others but also of the very process implied in teaching. It is impossible to teach without the courage to love, without the courage to try a thousand times before giving up. ... We must dare, in the full sense of the word, to speak of love without the fear of being called ridiculous, mawkish, or unscientific, if not antiscientific. We must dare in

---

2 See, for example, Freire (1983, 1996, pp. 62, 78–79, 1998b, p. 24, 28–29) and Horton and Freire (1990, pp. 23–27, 31–32).

order to say scientifically, and not as mere blah-blah-blah, that we study, we learn, we teach, we know with our entire body. We do all of these things with feeling, with emotion, with wishes, with fear, with doubts, with passion, and also with critical reasoning. However, we never study, learn, teach, or know with the last only. We must dare so as never to dichotomize cognition and emotion. (Freire, 1998b, p. 3)

Such statements hint at where Freire's thinking might have taken him had he been granted further writing years. It would be fair to say, however, that he does not provide quite the depth in analysis that these ideas seem to demand in his work. Freire opens doors for others, but he does not step through those doors and explore notions such as love and hope in the sort of critical detail necessary to fully understand their significance for his ethic or educational theory.

Pedagogical Imperialism?

I have argued, then, that Freire's epistemology might be described as essentialist and rationalist in only a restricted sense, and that while there was more work to do, Freire was committed to an expansive and holistic critical ideal in which reason and emotion would be radically integrated. Margonis raises further issues, however, that demand attention. He invites us to consider whether Freire's debt to Plato and the enlightenment faith in human reason leads toward a form of imperialism. This is related, in Freire's case, to pressing concerns about the nature of pedagogical intervention and the possibility of cultural invasion. C. A. Bowers is a pivotal figure in Margonis's critique, as he is in *Education, Literacy, and Humanization*. While I shall pose some problems in response to Margonis's analysis, I should stress that, overall, I find his comments helpful.

Freire, Margonis contends, inculcates a worldview that 'does not respect tradition' (Margonis, 2003, p. 149). I think this is inaccurate. Freire makes it plain that it is not tradition per se to which he is opposed but dogmatic adherence to, or unjustifiable compliance with, it. Freire is not 'against' tradition; rather, he is against social structures, practices, and relations which force people to accept tradition, or actively discourage them from questioning it, or prevent them from discovering alternative ways of viewing the world. He does not say that we should actively seek to overturn tradition or encourage others to do so. His argument is simply that we ought not to privilege traditional beliefs and practices over other beliefs and practices. All forms of cultural practice should, from a Freirean point of view, be open to questioning. This does not mean, however, that all beliefs, values, attitudes, practices, or social structures will be questioned all the time. Even in his earliest work, where his debt to enlightenment thinking is perhaps most obvious,

Freire says that critical consciousness is characterized by 'receptivity to the new for reasons beyond mere novelty and by the good sense not to reject the old just because it is old – by accepting what is valid in both old and new' (Freire, 1976, p. 18).

Margonis claims that Freire encourages analytical thinking through his educational programs as a means for assisting people to 'control their circumstances' (Margonis, 2003, p. 149). This is only partially true. Yes, Freire wants people to gain greater control over their lives; but complete control is never possible. Freire makes it clear that we are all shaped by our social, cultural, and historical circumstances. Our ideas and practices are never exclusively our own; we are, in a sense, always joint architects of our own destinies. Nor does Freire overestimate the role education or analytical thinking can play in changing social structures and relations of oppression. Education is vitally important, but it is always just one part of the wider process of social transformation.

Margonis accepts that my criticisms of Bowers' oversimplifications are justified, but argues that these criticisms 'do not completely discredit the contrasts Bowers articulates' (p. 150). He suggests that Bowers was 'pursuing questions of urgent significance' and that I am 'too quick to dismiss the plausibility of Bowers' argument' (p. 151). On one of these points, I can only say that I am full agreement with Margonis: Bowers was pursuing questions of urgent significance. In *Education, Literacy, and Humanization* I devote a full chapter exclusively to Bowers' work, and his ideas are also discussed elsewhere in the book (e.g. in my chapter on conscientization). I attempt to address Bowers' arguments respectfully and systematically. In the opening paragraphs of the chapter on Bowers I note that his work 'poses a formidable challenge for Freirean scholars and practitioners' (Roberts, 2000, p. 119), and offer the following remarks:

> Perhaps the greatest strength of Bowers' analysis lies in the significance of the questions he raises. For Bowers calls into question precisely those characteristics often most valued in Freirean education: critical reflection, the questioning of established beliefs and authority structures, the dialogical problematization of everyday life, and the commitment to social transformation. Bowers draws attention to one of the deepest concerns facing teachers, namely, the question of how their actions as educators might impact on the lives of their students. His work serves as a reminder that there is always a fine line between affirming and denying the experiences of others. In according the problem of intervention a central place in his investigation, Bowers anticipates later work by postmodern theorists on the dangers of attempting to speak for, or even with, others. Bowers thus addresses issues of fundamental importance for not only Freireans, but all educationists and, in this respect, his discussion is stimulating and helpful. (pp. 119–120)

I hope this passage gives some indication of the tone of my critique. I deal in considerable analytical detail with Bowers' arguments, and acknowledge the crucial importance of his work for Freirean scholars. I accept aspects of Bowers' position, noting for example, that his work 'is helpful in highlighting the sensitivities educationists must display in involving themselves in the lives of others' (p. 133). I agree, also, that whatever the flaws (as I see them) in Bowers' account of Freire's work, 'it is clear that Freire's orientation to the social world contrasts in important ways with that adopted by the Chipewyan and many other groups in traditional societies' (p. 135). I had no intention, then, of discrediting the contrasts Bowers makes. Instead, I acknowledge that there are differences but question whether some of them were of the kind depicted by Bowers. In the book I consider how Bowers put the contrasts to work in building his argument, and question both the substance and structure of that argument.

There is a good deal of philosophical discussion in *Education, Literacy, and Humanization* about the nature of pedagogical intervention generally and, more specifically, about the form of intervention advocated by Freire. Bowers observed that the Chipewyan try to avoid being in situations where established beliefs will be questioned. They place a high value on tradition and adopt an integrative approach to understanding themselves and their environment. They tend to learn by practical example rather than via manuals and step-by-step instructions. Some of these features of Chipewyan culture find a ready contrast with Freire's work. Freire emphasizes critical social action, dialogue and debate, the problematization of reality, and the right to question ideas and practices. As I point out in the book, however, Freire never, to the best of my knowledge, had any involvement with the Chipewyan people. In fact, as far as I am aware, he never offered any detailed written comment on them or their way of life. Bowers collapses complex and diverse intellectual traditions, practices, and ways of life into two clearly opposing groups: Western and non-Western. He places Freire squarely in the former camp, and construes him as a 'carrier' of a 'Western mind set.' The Chipewyan become the logical (non-Western) 'Other' in this equation, and Freire gains a form of 'guilt by association':

> Bowers aligns Freire with certain strands of Western thought, alludes to some of the problems in these views, and then asks, in effect, 'What if Freire's form of pedagogy were to be applied to the Chipewyan context?' Bowers then proceeds to show how Freirean theory and Chipewyan conceptions of reality do no comfortably mesh, and concludes that it would be problematic to 'use' Freire's pedagogy 'in an Islamic culture or one [such as the Chipewyan's] not already partially assimilated to the Western mind set' (Roberts, 2000, p. 123).

As Margonis notes, I find Bowers' clear-cut binary division between 'Western' and 'non-Western' simplistic and unhelpful. I also believe Bowers' talk of 'the' 'Western mind set' is highly problematic, and I see the depiction of Freire as a 'carrier' of this mind set as deeply flawed. But even if we leave these problems aside and accept that Freire's approach to understanding and living in the world differs in important ways from the culture and worldview of the Chipewyan, we have no reason to believe Freire would have wanted to have imposed his ideas, values and practices on the Chipewyan – or, indeed, on other indigenous groups elsewhere in the world. In both his published theoretical work and his conduct as an educational practitioner, Freire never conveyed the impression that he was interested in invading societies in this way. He stressed, as a constant theme running through his books, the importance of first attempting to understand the context and culture of those with whom we might work. He was invited to lead and contribute to educational programs and did not set himself up as a kind of pedagogical missionary seeking to 'convert' others to his way of life. Freire believed he had a right, in situations where he was invited to teach or to coordinate an educational program, to convey his own views, but he did not force them on others or act disrespectfully toward those who viewed the world through different cultural lenses.

Bowers was, as Margonis points out, 'an ecological thinker who … [was] deeply distrustful of western conceptions of human control over the earth' (pp. 149–150). He probably believed, Margonis surmises, 'that westerners should endeavor to learn the more respectful understanding of the earth and animals expressed by many Indigenous groups' (p. 150). I could not agree more that developing such an understanding is essential, and I believe we are indebted to Bowers for his work in this area. In the book I suggest that the 'elevation of human activity over all other forms of ecological life by some Westerners is arguably highly problematic. There is, as many Western thinkers (Bowers included) have recognized, much that might be learned from cultural groups other than our own' (Roberts, 2000, p. 133). Of course, there are groups within Western as well as non-Western cultures with long histories of commitment to a holistic and integrative relationship between human beings and the biotic environment. But this does not detract from the points made above. I could have said more about these issues in the book, as they are, in a world facing deep environmental and social problems, of vital importance. Bowers made a significant contribution to educational scholarship by bringing these questions to our attention. There is nothing in Freire's work, however, to suggest that he would have disagreed with Bowers about the seriousness of these problems. He too was genuinely concerned about the problems of pollution, the appalling physical conditions in our major cities, the arrogance of the quest by some groups to 'conquer' nature, and the destructive impact of capitalist production on the earth and its inhabitants. Freire's later work, in particular, makes it clear that these issues mattered a great deal to him (see especially, Freire, 1998a).

Bowers might have said that even if Freire felt this way, he failed to identify the deep cultural assumptions that lead to, or are consistent with, these ecological problems. This, in Bowers' view, was because Freire was trapped within the 'Western mind set' and was unable to recognize its influence on his philosophy and pedagogy. Bowers made claims of this kind as a Westerner, working within a 'Western' university, writing for 'Western' publications. While admitting that he had not escaped the conditioning effects of humanist ideology, he nonetheless seemed to imply that he had managed to step sufficiently outside this conditioning and the limits imposed by his own scholarly experience to provide a critique of the Western worldview that had shaped that experience. Yet, he appeared to regard Freire as a peculiarly unreflective intellectual – as someone so deeply immersed in 'the' Western mind set that he was utterly incapable of developing the sort of critical qualities Bowers himself displayed. Freire did not explore ecological questions in anything like the detail evidenced by Bowers' own work, but then neither did Bowers grapple at length with many of the philosophical, political and educational issues tackled by Freire. There is, we must surely all recognize, a limit to what we can all pursue – as both theorists and practitioners – with depth and conviction. Freire said less about these issues than Bowers, but what he does say – or imply – is, I think, less antithetical to the position Bowers supported than Bowers would have had us believe.

There is an omission in Margonis's summary of my argument about intervention that cannot escape comment. I should say firstly, however, that I agree with Margonis's useful restatement of the conclusion reached in one part of that argument, namely: that 'Chipewyan cultural norms allow for far less educational intervention than Anglo cultural norms' (p. 151). My objection is to the leap in logic implied by a remark about the 'linguistic' argument I mount in response to Bowers (p. 151). My argument is not merely a linguistic one, as Margonis claims, but also a substantive one. This is not, however, my main concern here. Margonis is largely accurate in his first claim: I do argue that any form of teaching (as Freire defines this term), or any system or program of education, will be necessarily interventionist. But it does not follow from this that 'Freire's style of intervention should be just as acceptable as Chipewyan styles of intervention' (p. 151). A case has to be made to demonstrate that Freirean intervention is justified. This is an important point, because it speaks to the key concern raised by Bowers about the possibility of education becoming a form of cultural invasion.

Not all forms of educational intervention are acceptable. If we accept that educational programs are necessarily interventionist, we face the heavy burden of showing how and why the differences we make as pedagogues might be justified. This is why I go to some lengths in the book to demonstrate that Freire's form of pedagogical intervention was, in the situations with which he was dealing, not only ethically defensible but arguably highly desirable. There is, then, a missing step in Margonis's account of the argument: if we accept that teaching and other forms of purposeful educational activity are interventionist, we must (I am using 'must' in the normative sense here) consider the form that intervention takes. To put this another way: the 'acceptability' or 'non-acceptability' of Freirean pedagogy – or any approach to pedagogy – cannot be derived merely from the fact that it is interventionist, but can only be assessed in the light of a theory of judgment which allows us to distinguish between different forms of intervention. I do not dispute Margonis's claim that the forms of intervention practiced by Freire differ from those practiced by the Chipewyan. I simply try to show in the book that Bowers distorts and simplifies the differences between the two approaches by portraying one as 'interventionist' and the other as 'noninterventionist.'

Education and Dilemmas of Difference

Margonis returns near the end of his essay to the faith – expressed through the ideals of reason, dialogue, or intelligence – enlightenment philosophers (and I think he includes Freire here) place in 'a process of producing truth that stands in opposition to dogma and tradition' (p. 152). The reference to 'dogma and tradition' seems like an odd coupling of terms to me. I agree that Freire and most other 'enlightenment philosophers' oppose dogma, but this does not mean they stand against tradition. As noted earlier in this chapter, Freire believed it was important to accept what is worthwhile in both the 'old' and the 'new.' He did not see all forms of social change as progressive, and he spoke with great fondness and passion about some of the traditions in his native Brazil. At the same time, he did not want to preserve all traditional practices and forms of social organization at all costs. Ensuring cultural survival was not, at the end of the day, his highest ethical principle. Freire would certainly have been devastated by the wiping out of traditional homelands and the erasure – by force – of opportunities for indigenous peoples to preserve, create, and recreate their cultures. But he would not have placed the imperative of preserving a culture ahead of his commitment to the ideal of humanization. For him, this was a universal human vocation. Where established structures and practices clearly impeded the pursuit of this vocation for some members of a cultural group, and were thus (from his perspective) dehumanizing, he was not afraid to express his opposition to them.

Margonis observes that while 'Marxists may believe in wiping the slate clean of old beliefs which sanction oppression, ... many Indigenous peoples are devoted to the maintenance of cultures that show little commitment to democracy or socialism' (p. 152). It is not especially helpful, or accurate, to describe Freire as a 'Marxist.' This is not to deny the influence of Marx on aspects of Freire's work. Freire's debt to Marx is evident in his ontology and his epistemology, and his ethical position too owes much to his reading of this great thinker. Freire was committed to a form of participatory democracy along broadly socialist lines. He accepted, however, as Margonis does, that not everyone shared his ethical and political ideals. His stance is not one of 'wiping the slate clean' of old beliefs; rather, it is a matter of forging new beliefs in the light of a critical assessment of the old ones. It is not, from a Freirean standpoint, possible to deny one's history or circumstances – or to leave past beliefs entirely behind us. There is, instead, a dynamism at work – a dialectical relationship – between the 'old' and the 'new.' We continue to be shaped by past events and ideas, even in the midst of a process in which we seek to criticize and repudiate those events and ideas. We encounter new challenges, question traditional views or existing practices, and from this a synthesis of the two emerges. In this sense, there is always both change and continuity.

Margonis argues, correctly in my view, that good examples of 'hybrid' pedagogies – incorporating elements of Indigenous practice and Freirean principles – can be found (p. 153). In fact, I am fortunate to have a prime example on my 'front doorstep' in New Zealand.[3] Many Māori scholars in the field of Education acknowledge their debt to Freire. They have, as Graham Hingangaroa Smith (1999) has argued, integrated Freirean ideas with their own political practice. Smith identifies three key notions in Freire's work: conscientization, resistance, and transformative praxis. While a technocratic interpretation of Freire's work would construe these as linear, sequential steps to be followed in the process of liberation, Smith represents each element in the form of a cycle. He maintains that many Māori frequently become active in indigenous politics before encountering Freirean theory. Māori have actively resisted the dominant ideology of schooling in New Zealand, and have transformed the educational landscape in this country with a series of intervention strategies. These include Te Kohanga Reo ('language nests') at the preschool level, Kura Kaupapa Māori at primary (elementary) school level, and Waananga at the tertiary education (college) level. Smith observes:

> A key understanding here with respect to the relationship between Māori resistance and Freire's ideas, is that Māori did not go out and buy Freire's book and then apply

---

3   See also Kee and Carr-Chellman (2019).

his ideas as some kind of recipe for liberation and emancipation. On the contrary, most Māori (and this was certainly my own experience) came to Freire after they were well involved in resistance and struggle. The point is that for many Māori, Freire's writings provided support, direction, validity and confirmation of what they were already doing. (p. 36)

Against an instrumentalist view of conscientization, resistance, and transformative praxis, Smith maintains: 'Māori experience tends to suggest that these elements may occur in any order and indeed may all occur simultaneously.' This alternative model provides a more inclusive structure, and suggests that 'everyone is "in the struggle" to some extent' (p. 40).

While much of Margonis's discussion is devoted to the challenges raised by Bowers, he also comments, with considerable insight, on Ellsworth's well-known critique of critical pedagogy (Ellsworth, 1989). I agree with much of what Margonis has to say here and wish to address just a few matters of theoretical detail. I would, firstly, want to draw a distinction between a commitment to solidarity – which is important to Freire – and acceptance of a 'vanguardist' role for critical educators. Freire sometimes leaves himself open (especially in *Pedagogy in Process*: Freire, 1978) to criticisms of vanguardism when he speaks about the role of revolutionary (and educational) leaders. It is not difficult to see why the notion of an elite intellectual vanguard leading 'the masses' or 'the people' along an educative path might be considered objectionable. Freire did not see intellectuals as necessarily part of 'an elite,' and he never intended to construe liberating education as a process of one enlightened group lifting another group upwards or away from their ignorance. Solidarity demands a genuine care for and commitment to others and to some sort of shared goal. In the specifically Freirean sense, it also implies a willingness – indeed, an eagerness – to enter into dialogue with others, and to engage in process of collective struggle against oppression. An 'elitist' conception of vanguardism might be regarded as anti-dialogical, and thus stands in tension with the Freirean notion of solidarity.

Margonis applauds Ellsworth for being 'unwilling to feel too confident that she is working in her students' political interests,' (p. 154) but in this respect, she does not differ substantially from Freire. Freire often warned against the dangers of being too certain of one's certainties, and urged teachers to reflect continuously on their actions, attitudes, beliefs, and commitments. Ellsworth has the courage to admit that she was not sure how she should act in the face of multiple, often-conflicting layers of oppression (across class, race, gender, age, sexuality, and other lines) in the classroom. Yet, Ellsworth's work also poses some significant problems, that continue to be debated in our present day. It is hard to know what we might mean by 'interests' if we accept Ellsworth's argument, and it is thus difficult to know how we might obtain greater confidence that student interests are being served. Ellsworth argues that appeals to universal philosophical propositions (including ethical principles) have been oppressive to those who are not 'European, White, male, middle class, Christian, able-bodied, thin, and heterosexual' (Ellsworth, 1989, p. 304). It is not clear from Ellsworth's account what it is that makes something oppressive, or what 'interests' need to be served if a less oppressive reality is to emerge. Given her critique of universals, Ellsworth does not want to – perhaps cannot (logically) – provide a theory of oppression or a notion of human interests that might go beyond the demands of the diverse groups to which she refers. We can accept that those demands are legitimate, but Ellsworth does not provide the theoretical resources for us to know why we ought to do so. Ellsworth believes her understanding of racism will necessarily be constrained by her 'white skin and middle-class privilege' (p. 308), and, in the face of contradictions, conflicts, and tensions in her classroom, she reaches a state of what might be called 'pedagogical paralysis.'

Freire would, I think, have admired Ellsworth's honesty in revealing her difficulties, and would have agreed with her that we must acknowledge 'learned and internalized oppressions' (Ellsworth, 1989, p. 308) such as racism, sexism, and classism. He would also have accepted that getting involved – as we must, in one way or another, in all classroom situations – with student lives is a complex and challenging process. We must acknowledge, as Freire often did, that our actions as teachers have consequences for the lives of others and proceed with great care in working with students of difference. This does not have to mean that we should, as Margonis puts it, 'disown' the views we have been raised with (p. 154). I suspect Freire would have said that we can never completely shed the cloak of past experiences, attitudes and beliefs. To be sure, we must seek ways to identify, understand, address, and overcome our prejudices, but this is more a process of 'owning up' to – and going beyond – our failings than of 'disowning' them. In *Education, Literacy, and Humanization* I conclude my discussion of differences (and similarities) between Ellsworth and Freire with these words:

> If it is Ellsworth who draws our attention to difficulties associated with addressing the question, 'What ought I (or we) to do?', it is Freire who reminds us that this question can still be answered, even if only in provisional and contingent ways. On the Freirean view, taking a risk-laden, potentially contradictory, always constrained stand against oppression is almost invariably preferable to taking no stand at all. (Roberts, 2000, p. 109)

Margonis is on the mark, in my view, when he says that we need to search for theories that 'help us understand both the obstacles to dialogue and the potential for solidarity' across differences (p. 155). In this respect, I believe we would be well served by further work on the relationship between 'universals' and 'particulars' in understanding and addressing oppression and liberation. Post-structuralist and postmodern theorists in Education and other fields have played a key role in helping us to confront these questions, but we must remain open to other ways – including those drawn from indigenous communities and the neglected esoteric traditions in a variety of cultures – of continuing our conversations on these issues. I wish to thank Frank Margonis for allowing me to rethink some of the fundamental philosophical claims in *Education, Literacy, and Humanization*, and for encouraging further critical discussion of major themes in Freire's work.

CHAPTER SIX

Education, Ethics, and Leadership

Camus, Freire, and Covid-19

By early 2020, news had spread around the world of a potentially devastating viral outbreak. The virus was said to have originated in a market in Wuhan, China, near the end of 2019, and within a matter of weeks the first 'lockdown' was imposed. Suddenly, references to the 'Corona virus' seemed to be everywhere. By the time it had become widely known as 'Covid-19,' the virus had already started to appear in other parts of the world and there was a growing realization that a global crisis was unfolding. The World Health Organisation, after some initial hesitation, eventually declared that what we were facing was a pandemic, and one country after another began to implement large-scale public health measures to contain the spread of the virus. As the months went by, the number of deaths from the virus kept rising at an alarming rate. Hospitals struggled to cope with burgeoning numbers of seriously ill patients. Pressure to develop a vaccine as quickly as possible began to mount, and trials of the various options that emerged were accelerated. Travel within and between countries became increasingly difficult, meetings moved online, and systems for more closely monitoring the movements of citizens were introduced. Public briefings from politicians and officials became more frequent, and terms such as 'social distancing' and 'contact tracing' entered the language of everyday life.

For some people, there was, under lockdown conditions, more than the usual amount of time available for activities such as reading. One of the books to which many turned was Albert Camus's *The Plague*. Already widely regarded as a classic of 20th century literature, *The Plague* (Camus, 1960) has now became even more significant. For in the pages of this memorable novel, Camus describes a situation with many similarities to the conditions created by the Covid-19 pandemic. It did not take long for references to the book to begin appearing in newspapers, magazines, blogs, and academic journals.[1] This chapter adds to this body of work but with a distinctive focus. In the pages that follow, both the Covid-19 pandemic and Camus's novel will be considered in the light of ideas from Paulo Freire. As has been noted elsewhere (Schugurensky, 2011), Freire's work has frequently been compared with that of other thinkers. To date, however, little attention has been paid to links between Freire and Camus. It will be argued here that in the stance adopted and actions taken by the central character of the novel, Dr Bernard Rieux, we see an exemplification of many of the virtues espoused by Freire, and much can be learned from his example in reflecting on the current Covid-19 crisis.

A Literary Case Study: Camus's *The Plague*

When he sat down to begin composing the novel that would become *The Plague*, Albert Camus had already gained considerable acclaim for his work as a writer. Camus was born in Algeria but spent much of his adult life in France. He was, with Jean-Paul Sartre and Simone de Beauvoir, one of the best known Parisian intellectuals of the 1940s and 1950s. His wrote both fiction and non-fiction. His early novel *The Stranger* (Camus, 1989) had attracted great interest. Other well-known works in Camus' corpus include *The Fall* (Camus, 2000), the stories collected in *Exile and the Kingdom* (Camus, 1991a), and the plays *Caligula*, *The Misunderstanding*, and *The Just* (Camus, 1958). Camus also adapted Dostoevsky's *The Possessed* (sometimes translated as *Demons* or *The Devils*) and Faulkner's *Requiem for a Nun* for the stage. His influential philosophical work, *The Myth of Sisyphus* (Camus, 1991b), with its famous opening statement, has been a common reference point for existentialist inquiry: 'There is but one truly serious philosophical problem,' Camus begins, 'and that is suicide'; 'Judging whether life is or is not worth living amounts to answering the fundamental question of philosophy' (p. 3). Camus also published many other essays on political and ethical themes, together with journalistic reports and shorter commentaries (Camus, 1968, 1991c, 1995).

---

1 E.g., Earle (2020), Kabel and Phillipson (2021), Lachenal and Thomas (2020), Novacevski (2021), Rosenthal (2020), Salcedo (2020), Stelson (2021), Unuajohwofia and Orhero (2021), Vandekerckhove (2020), and Zaretsky (2020a, b).

He was awarded the Nobel Prize for Literature in 1957. The almost-complete manuscript for the strongly autobiographical and most overtly educational of his books, *The First Man*, was found in the wreckage of the car accident in which he died and was finally released by his daughter for publication in the 1990s (Camus, 1996). The details of his life and death have been well-documented in several major biographies published over the last few decades (e.g., Bronner, 1999; Hawes, 2009; Todd, 2000; Zaretsky, 2010).

Educational readings of Camus have been available for more than fifty years, but there has been a particularly strong level of interest since the turn of the century. In some cases (Hobson, 2017; Roberts, Gibbons, & Heraud, 2015), these have been book-length studies, with chapters on a range of works, fictional and non-fictional, across Camus's oeuvre. There are also now many articles on Camus in educational journals and edited collections, addressing questions of ontology and morality (Denton, 1964; Oliver, 1973), the implications of Camus's work for teaching and learning (Gallchóir & McGarr, 2021; Gordon, 2016; Götz, 1987; Roberts, 2008a), the connections between his ideas and the development of communities of inquiry (Burgh & Thornton, 2016), his relevance to early childhood education and children's literature (Gibbons, 2012; Phillips, 2020), the concept of exile as a way of thinking about inclusion (Brady, 2017), and the pedagogical and philosophical significance of notions of suicide (Thornton, 2019; Weddington, 2007). Camus has been seen as helpful in demonstrating the value of literature for philosophical inquiry in education (Marshall, 2008; Roberts, 2008b). *The Plague* has received direct attention from educationists, both before the current Covid-19 pandemic (Gibbons, 2013a, b) and during it (Murillo, 2021; Peters, 2020; Williams, 2020). The book has also been engaged by scholars from a range of other fields, with much of this scholarship focusing on the ethical, political and theological dimensions of the work (Davis, 2007; Fendt, 2019, 2020; Krapp, 1999; Principe, 2020; Sharpe, 2016b). The lessons in the novel for health professionals have also been explored (Tuffuor & Payne, 2017), and Camus's silences on matters of ethnicity and gender in have been noted (Lund, 2011).

The Plague is Camus's longest novel and was originally published (as *La Peste*) in 1947. It is set in Oran, a French port town in Algeria, and its central character is Bernard Rieux, a doctor. Other key characters include Tarrou (a visitor to the town, with whom Rieux forms a friendship), Rambert (a journalist), Grand (a clerk), Cottard (a secretive figure, involved in various shady dealings), and Father Paneloux (a Jesuit priest). As the action of the novel unfolds, a story with many similarities to the current Covid-19 crisis emerges. An early sign that something may be wrong in Oran is the appearance on city streets of rats that start dying in large numbers. Shortly thereafter, the first human cases of a mysterious illness begin to emerge. Concern is expressed in some quarters, but authorities attempt to play down the crisis, and many act as if it is 'business as usual.' People start to die from the new illness, and keep dying in ever greater numbers. Bureaucratic impediments slow the response to an increasingly disturbing situation. Information is released, but only in limited doses. A growing awareness of the seriousness of the situation develops, and among citizens and health professionals, the word 'plague' begins to be uttered. Sick individuals are isolated, then the entire town is closed off. New regulations are put in place and martial law is imposed. There is a rationing of goods and electricity. Fatalities keep rising rapidly. Hospitals are unable to cope and auxiliary wards are created to deal with the overflowing increase in patients. Commercial activities are reduced, though cafés, bars, and picture theaters remain open. There are fewer cars on roads and ships in port. Communication with the outside world is inhibited. There is a separation of families from dying loved ones. Mass graves are created. Feelings of bewilderment, anxiety, loneliness, frustration, anger, and despair are expressed, but there are also plenty of examples of selflessness, sacrifice, kindness, and solidarity. Rieux and others involved in caring for the sick work tirelessly. They put in long hours, under extremely testing conditions, living with constant exhaustion. The numbers falling ill gradually begin to decline. There is a sense of elation as the opening up of the town is announced. The novel closes with an indication that life will return to 'normal,' but with a warning that plagues will emerge again in the future (Camus, 1960).

The Plague can be seen as a prophetic account of how a crisis of the kind we have witnessed in 2020 and 2021 might develop and evolve. Some have also read the novel as an allegory of the Nazi occupation of France. But this work of fiction also has much to teach us about education, ethics, and leadership. Rieux undertakes his medical duties quietly and attentively, with a genuine sense of care and concern for those who are suffering. He starts from a position of humility. When faced with a looming crisis, he does not assume he 'knows it all'; rather, he seeks to know more, adopting an open, investigative posture. He acknowledges his uncertainties. His focus is on the task at hand, and on the welfare of others, rather than on the promptings of his own ego. He is fair-minded and even-handed in his dealings with patients, family members, and friends. He demonstrates the ability to listen and to learn. He has the courage to face the reality of the situation. He is also deeply committed to his duties, with an extremely taxing work schedule. He recognizes, nonetheless, that he is not alone and senses the need to reach out to others. He realizes that the plague is a shared burden. He builds friendships with others who volunteer their help in the midst of the crisis. He is calm and considered in his demeanor but also willing to speak up and to fight for what is important. He is a leader in his manner and bearing – in the virtues he exhibits, the decisions he makes, and the actions he takes. He displays these qualities not just for the short term, but consistently, over many months. Rieux's virtues are remarkably similar to those espoused by Freire for progressive teachers. The next section elaborates on these connections and reflects on the current Covid-19 crisis in the light of this analysis.

Teaching, Leadership, and Hope: Ethics and Education in Times of Crisis

The model of leadership conveyed, implicitly, by Rieux is not one of grand gestures. Rather, its focus is on the everyday; on the smallest, often largely invisible moments of human action and interaction. As Rieux says at one point in the novel, in conversation with Rambert and Tarrou, 'there's no question of heroism in all this. It's a matter of common decency' (Camus, 1960, p. 158). When asked to explain what he means by 'common decency,' Rieux replies: 'I don't know what it means for other people. But in my case I know that it consists in doing my job' (p. 158). This is an approach to leadership built on the principle of commitment, on the idea of *work*. Later, Rieux says: '… you know, I feel more fellowship with the defeated than with saints. Heroism and sanctity don't really appeal to me, … What interests me is being a man' (p. 245). Near the end of the book, we discover that the hitherto unnamed narrator of the tale is none other than Rieux himself. We are told that Rieux had decided to chronicle the events in Oran 'so that he should not be one of those who hold their peace but should bear witness in favor of those plague-stricken people' (pp. 296–297). His account would serve as a 'memorial' to the 'injustice and outrage' they faced (p. 297). There is also a conclusion with educational implications offered in these final observations: that 'what we learn in a time of pestilence … [is] that there are more things to admire in men than to despise' (p. 297). He is aware that this would not be a tale of a final victory and that similar horrors would await others in the future. We will again need those who, despite their own afflictions, will, without trying to be saints, refuse to 'bow down to pestilences' and 'strive their utmost to be healers' (p. 297).

Freire speaks of humility as one of the key virtues of a progressive teacher. 'To be humble,' he says, 'does not mean to be afraid of doing things'; to the contrary, '[t]o be humble pushes me towards acting without thinking that by acting I am the best' (Freire, 1995, p. 19). A posture of humility grows from a recognition that we are all in the process of becoming, necessarily incomplete as human beings. Being humble means not being afraid to be criticized but also not being 'full of yourself because some people said you are interesting' (p. 19). Humility requires an honest assessment of our faults – and our abilities. Our virtues are not given to us at birth; rather, we have to create them. Humility is a 'strong exercise we have to practise in every moment of our life. It is an exercise which implies some courage' (p. 19). Rieux is, in many respects, the very embodiment of the quality of humility, as this is understood by Freire. His humility both grows from and nurtures his inquiring mind. When faced with the unusual spectacle of rats dying in Oran's streets, he is at once curious and concerned. He wants to know more, but not simply by being told what to believe by others. He adopts an investigative stance, paying attention, gathering evidence, and listening to others, while also drawing on his medical knowledge and experience. Humility in Freirean theory is closely related to the idea of openness, and this too is a key feature of Rieux's orientation to life, both personally and professionally. When faced with an unfamiliar, perplexing or challenging situation, he avoids the temptation to become reactionary or defensive, fearful, or aggressive. He displays an openness to learning more, and has the humility necessary for the process of discovery. There is a constant interplay between what he knows and what he does not know, and this is consistent with Freire's conception of education.

In his later work, Freire also emphasized the importance of tolerance, and again, Rieux models this virtue. For Freire, '[t]olerance is the quality of creating something against certain dimensions of ourselves. It is the ability to enjoy difference. It is to learn from the difference. It means not to consider ourselves better than others precisely because they are different from us' (p. 21). Being tolerant does not mean giving up our own commitments and dreams; nor does it imply uncritical acceptance of the views expressed by others. To be tolerant is not to be 'indifferent or irresponsible' (p. 22). But being prepared to listen to others, respectfully and attentively, is essential if we are to put our own ideas to the test. We may disagree with a colleague or student but there is no place in Freirean education for outright, unreflective dismissal of what others have to say. At the same time, in exercising tolerance for difference, we must not tacitly endorse the right for others to behave disrespectfully or aggressively toward others. As Freire (1998b) puts it, '[b]eing tolerant does not mean acquiescing to the intolerable' (p. 42). Tolerance for Freire is more than *tolerating*. If our attitude is one of doing someone a favor by putting up with them, we are demonstrating hypocrisy, not tolerance (p. 42).

Rieux acknowledges the differences he sees between himself and others who have their own distinctive responsibilities and commitments in Oran during the period of the plague. He never adopts a condescending air in his dealings with fellow inhabitants of the town, and the patience he displays is not merely for show. It emerges from his genuine sense of care for those with whom he associates, both professionally and socially. Through listening to what others have to say, he deepens his understanding of himself. His friendship with Tarrou helps to lighten the load for both men, their brief escape to converse and swim in the sea providing a sense of temporary relief in the midst of the ongoing crisis. Rieux builds a strong dialogical relationship with Tarrou. The latter is sometimes the more talkative of the two but there is an easy exchange of views and a breaking down of some of the formal barriers that are in place in institutional environments. Rieux is also respectful of Father Paneloux's explanation of events in Oran, and of his stoicism in the face of his own death from the plague. He can see that there is a consistency between the message the Father conveys on the pulpit and the way he lives, and dies, in the world. He is nonetheless clear that his own views are not the same as the preacher's. He is so busy attending to others that he has little time to consider his own fate. He is an atheist, and his hope lies not in eternal salvation but in the resilience of human beings in the face of adversity. He cannot accept that the intense suffering of a child in the clutches of the plague is 'God's will.' '[U]ntil my dying day,' he says to the priest, 'I shall refuse to love a scheme of things in which children are put to torture' (p. 208). At the same time, in his actions there is arguably tacit endorsement for one theme developed in a sermon by Father Paneloux, namely, the idea that suffering can be a *teacher*. As a doctor administering to the sick, and as the narrator of the novel, Rieux demonstrates the importance of learning from the plague. Covid-19 can have educative value for us, in a similar way. It can enhance our appreciation for what we have, sharpen our sense of what matters most, and reaffirm our commitment to each other.

Freire speaks of decisiveness as a virtue. This is not a bull-headed determination to act, nor is it a hurried attempt to do things without adequate thought. Freire acknowledges that we may have doubts and questions. Indeed, as we have seen in earlier chapters, the principle of being less certain of one's certainties is fundamental to his pedagogical orientation. But having doubts, and expressing them, is not the same as being unable to make decisions. It takes courage to acknowledge that we are uncertain; equally courageous, however, is a decision to act, on the basis of careful deliberation and dialogue, even where such doubts exist. To 'do nothing' is not to be neutral; it is to allow the status quo to remain. In that sense, doing nothing is also doing something. Our decisions, including those that amount to leaving arrangements as they are, all have consequences. While we can never, in human affairs, predict exactly what those consequences will be, we can take responsibility for the part we play in shaping patterns of thought and action. This point is especially significant when considering the roles teachers play in guiding students. Every utterance a teacher makes in a classroom, every decision she or he makes about curriculum content or pedagogy, plays a part in opening up or inhibiting possibilities for student learning. Teachers can, and should, show that they are vulnerable; that they have weaknesses as well as strengths. They can confess that they have doubts and questions that cannot be easily answered. But a teacher must still *teach*, and not simply 'facilitate.' As Freire argues, 'although they [teachers] cannot take sole responsibility for the lives of their students, they must not, in the name of democracy, evade responsibility for making decisions' (p. 43). This is consistent with the Freirean idea, discussed elsewhere in this book, of exercising authority without being authoritarian.

Rieux goes about his job systematically and conscientiously, maintaining a certain professional distance, but without losing his 'human touch' as a doctor. The distance he establishes between himself and the tasks he has to complete is necessary in enabling him to continue working long hours, day after day, under extremely difficult conditions. This is part of the process of 'doing one's job,' to which Rieux refers when explaining what he means by 'decency.' Care for others also necessitates care for oneself. Of course, this self-care will often be compromised in crisis situations, but it is important to retain sufficient clarity to recognize signs of danger in one's mental, emotional, and physical state. Listlessness and a loss of a sense of purpose and direction in one's activities may signal a need to step back temporarily, in order to return to one's duties with renewed vigor and enthusiasm. It is, however, often when we are most at risk of developing this kind of deep fatigue that we cannot gain the perspective we need. That is partly why collegiality and trust in others – to care for us, as we will care for them – can be so important. Others can sometimes see changes in attitude or character that may, at a certain point when the pressure becomes too great, be less than obvious to a person him- or herself. Trusting colleagues to say what needs to be said, and to do what needs to be done, in our best interests, can be vital.

The ideal of 'decency' articulated and upheld by Rieux is consistent with Freire's educational and ethical ideals. Freire stresses the need for teachers to do their jobs well. Teaching is a demanding process, requiring a profound, holistic commitment of oneself to others and to the task at hand. Teachers need to care for the students and the colleagues with whom they work but they are also responsible to their discipline. They need to prepare thoroughly, know their subject areas comprehensively and critically, and have a sophisticated understanding of pedagogy. For Freire, teaching demands deep reflection on what is being taught, to whom, how, and why. Rigor is vital in the teaching process. We must, from a Freirean perspective, be true to our subject matter and to ourselves. We should not need, nor want, to believe that our truth is the only possible truth, but neither should we abandon the idea of truth altogether – as if any view of the world is as good as any other. There is an integrity that must be upheld through the act of teaching, regardless of the challenges posed by the educational setting in which we are working. This resonates with the stance adopted by Rieux, who after a brief interaction with Rambert, affirms his commitment to an ethical and epistemological ideal that would 'have no truck with injustice and compromises with the truth' (p. 10). Rieux does not feel a need to expound upon his views in elaborate detail; he shows what he stands for through his actions and interactions. He is calm but determined; open yet decisive. He quietly gets on with his job, without expecting recognition or reward for doing so. He is responsible rather than accountable, doing what he believes is right, without having to be cajoled by others. He often goes well beyond the 'call of duty,' working long hours, undertaking numerous small tasks that are hidden from official view but significant in making the lives of those who are suffering more bearable.

The Plague shows that there is a need for hope, even in the most despairing of situations. Indeed, as has been argued elsewhere (Roberts, 2016), it precisely in such situations that hope, as it were, 'comes into its own,' becoming all the more meaningful given the harrowing circumstances in which it must be nurtured. In the desperate conditions created by Covid-19, hope has emerged, in part, through the development of a number of different vaccines. As the more infectious and deadly Delta variant of the virus has spread across the globe, the call for widespread vaccination, in the hope that this will provide 'herd immunity,' has grown ever louder. Lockdowns have continued to be imposed but politicians, public health officials, and researchers have increasingly accepted that total elimination of the virus is unlikely. Now, the focus is more on learning to live with it, while significantly reducing the harm it causes. Vaccination is seen by most as a crucial element in this process. It is recognized by many that this is a problem that must be faced collectively, and that receiving the necessary injections is not just a matter of personal protection but is for the good of others as well. Nonetheless, there are people who, for various reasons, are resistant to being vaccinated. In some cases, there are legitimate medical reasons for this; in other cases, however, decisions are based on misinformation, often circulated via social media. With more time than ever being spent online during periods of lockdown, it is not hard to see how quickly ideas can spread and take a hold over consciousnesses. Already frustrated by the denial of freedoms that have long been taken for granted, there is among some citizens a propensity to lash out in anger at those responsible for the new rules and restrictions. The 'anti-vaccination movement' is, in reality, not a single, coherent movement at all and is often driven by sentiments that are 'anti' much more than vaccination. Whatever the reasons beyond these acts of refusal, there is no denying the strength of feeling among some groups. With laws now in place compelling vaccination in some industries and professions, the potential for separation and alienation of some groups from others seems greater than ever. This moment in the unfolding social history of the virus poses some searching ethical and educational questions. What might Freire – or Rieux – have done, faced with a situation of this kind?

From a Freirean perspective, as has been noted elsewhere in this book, the role of the educationist is not to impose his or her views on others. Intervention might be justified on public health grounds, but Freire would have argued that policy decisions also need to rest on sound ethical and pedagogical foundations. Compulsion of certain kinds under crisis conditions can be defended, but far better is a situation where citizens are involved throughout as active, critical participants in the design and implementation of policy initiatives. Politicians, policy-makers and citizens can all learn much – about themselves and about the problems being addressed – through such collective efforts, but this ideal can quickly break down in the face of fixed, firm beliefs. It is not enough to appeal to reason, for often sound arguments and empirical evidence appear to make little difference, especially where vaccination programs are seen as part of a wider conspiracy. Freire placed a premium on the importance of educational dialogue, but in some circumstances, the prospects for building the kind of pedagogical conversation he had in mind appear to be rather limited. Communication can, at times, seem to be difficult, if not impossible, with no obvious way to bridge the gap between people who adhere to very different positions or worldviews. Adopting a posture of openness may be a good starting point, but if educative dialogue is to proceed, this cannot be confined to one person or party in the conversation. Being prepared to stay silent for a period, and to simply listen, can also help. As Simone Weil (1997, 2001) counseled, if we are to develop our human capacity for attention, we need to learn how to watch and to wait. But waiting is the last thing many citizens in a Covid-19 world want to do. After multiple periods of lockdown, a certain weariness sets in, and people long for a return to 'normality.' Acknowledging this, and trying to understand how such circumstances shape perceptions and feelings, can be of value. Again, however, it must be noted that this may not produce any immediate results in advancing an educational conversation. Recognizing these limits to dialogue (and there are others not considered here) does not mean there is no point, from an educational perspective, in attempting to understand and engage with others.

We should, as Rieux would say, continue doing our jobs, with a calm, clear sense of focus and purpose, regardless of the obstacles we come up against. But more than this, the emergence of polarized positions on matters such as vaccination can, potentially at least, be seen as an educative moment for educators. For teachers at all levels, and especially in tertiary contexts, learning more about what students believe, and why, can be instructive. It can inform decisions we make about what and how to teach, influencing the recommendations we make for reading and the forms of assessment we employ. The existence of views radically at odds with our own can also prompt a reconsideration of our own assumptions. In 'reconsidering,' we may return to the position from which we started, but with a deeper appreciation of why we hold the views we do. Even if we conclude, on the basis of continuing reflection and research, that the current vaccination drive is not part of a wider conspiracy, this does not mean the tendency to think in conspiratorial terms is always misguided. There are, it must be acknowledged, plenty of examples throughout human history of powerful people conspiring to manipulate, control, dominate, and deter. It can be a helpful exercise to ask ourselves why we *don't* think a nationwide vaccination program is a conspiracy, and, as part of this process of inquiry, to ponder who might stand to gain, and how, from a public health initiative of this kind. It is not difficult to see how multinational pharmaceutical companies have a demonstrable interest in promoting their vaccines, but there is also merit in critically considering the other measures that have been put in place to combat the virus. Concerns over increasing surveillance, with the monitoring of citizens' movements via scanning applications and the like, need to be taken seriously. The Freirean intellectual virtues of curiosity, rigor, and an investigative frame of mind can serve us well in such situations. Again, the conclusion may not be that Covid-19 surveillance measures constitute a well-conceived, deliberate, orchestrated campaign to control or dominate or harm others, but the process of inquiry is itself worthwhile from an educational point of view.

Conclusion

In reflecting on how we might respond to the current global Covid-19 crisis, and on what we can learn from it, no one discipline or field has all the answers. More than ever, we need to respect the insights that can be gained from multiple areas of inquiry, across the sciences, humanities, and other domains. Research by educationists responding to the pandemic need not confine itself to data generated through empirical investigation or to works of theory; literature also has much to offer in pondering the ethical, pedagogical and political questions raised by this crisis. There is much to admire in the fictional figure of Rieux, but he is not 'perfect' – as is the case for all leaders. A similar point must be stressed when reading Freire. Freire was, as he insisted himself, an incomplete, imperfect being. His account of the virtues of progressive teachers is helpful in reflecting on ideals to which we might aspire in our own pedagogy. But the particulars of our time and place must always be carefully considered. We should not attempt to simply transpose a model of leadership or teaching from one context to another. Both Camus and Freire remind us of the complex ethical dilemmas we face in negotiating the challenges posed by everyday life, under both so-called 'normal' circumstances and in times of crisis. In the 'real' world, as in fiction, difficult decisions need to be made, and suffering cannot always be avoided. There are problems addressed (but not 'resolved') in *The Plague* that are also relevant to our age. There is, it can be argued, a need to attain a sense of the 'bigger picture' (e.g., via statistics) without losing sight of individuals and particulars. Among those on the 'front line' of our defenses against the pandemic, and particularly those in the health professions, a certain detachment must sometimes be cultivated – as a 'survival strategy' – but this need not become an attitude of indifference. This has been a tragic and turbulent moment in world history but the Covid-19 pandemic has also provided opportunities to learn, to grow, and to go on – with a sense of gritty hope in the face of the uncertainties that lie ahead.

CHAPTER SEVEN

Conscientization, Compassion, and Madness

Freire, Barreto, and the Limits of Education

Over the last two decades, a number of scholars have considered aspects of Paulo Freire's work from an aesthetic point of view. Lewis (2011), for example, critiques Freire's use of Francisco Brenand's artwork in adult literacy education, arguing that '[t]he ten existential illustrations Freire employs in his literacy program are reduced to nothing more than preparation for democracy after literacy is established—after the image is conquered by the word' (p. 42). Lewis sees Jacques Rancière's 'aesthetics of dissensus' as a promising alternative in rethinking the role of images in critical pedagogy (p. 38). Bingham (2016), also influenced by Rancière, addresses the theme of 'spectatorship' in Freirean theory, tracing debates over watching and seeing back to Plato and Aristotle. He compares Freire with Dewey, identifying differences between the two thinkers on the role of the spectator in the realm of art, while finding both to be 'anti-watching' in their educational positions. Bingham problematizes Freire's stance on spectatorship, connecting this with the 'tendency among educators to link pedagogy to the one best way to be human' (p. 191). A third example is provided by Todd (2018), who contrasts Freire's portrait of cultural action in the context of revolutionary education with Raymond Williams's emphasis on the 'ordinariness' of culture. She argues that, together, 'their views of culture allow us to hold the tension between practices of education as they already exist and the purposes of education as something more than preservation of custom' (p. 971). Todd continues: 'the explicitly emancipatory emphasis of Freire's idea of culture speaks more directly to how reorganizing traditional meanings and symbolic forms of expression actually effects change in the world. There is thus, an explicit aesthetic to Freire's work that complements what is at stake in seeing educational practices as "ordinary"' (p. 971).

Another avenue in bringing aesthetic questions more to the fore in reading Freire, critically but constructively, is via engagement with fiction. Over the last two decades, the value of literature for philosophical and educational inquiry has been widely acknowledged. Such recognition can take at least two different forms. One approach is to make the building of a case for literature the major focus; another is to show what fiction has to offer by reflecting on specific novels or short stories in the light of a given thinker's ideas. Freirean theory lends itself particularly well to the latter approach.[1] There is much in Freire's educational philosophy that can be helpful in our reading of a fictional work; similarly, in engaging fiction, we can deepen our understanding of key Freirean principles. These dual possibilities become evident in reflecting on his countryman Lima Barreto's novel, *The Sad End of Policarpo Quaresma* (Barreto, 2011). Barreto's work has received comparatively little attention in the English-speaking world. Even in his own country, Barreto was, for many decades after his death, treated as a marginal figure in Brazilian literature (Aidoo & Silva, 2013, p. 1). Today, however, he is regarded as 'one of Brazil's most published and debated authors' and *The Sad End of Policarpo Quaresma* is considered to be 'his most important work' (Serra, 2011, pp. 28, 37). The novel is both a searching examination of a country undergoing political change and a nuanced study of human fragilities.[2] This chapter focuses principally on the second of these two dimensions, and considers Barreto's central character from a Freirean perspective. I argue that while Freirean theory allows us to adopt a compassionate stance in seeking to understand Policarpo Quaresma, the ethical and pedagogical questions raised by his 'madness' find no easy answers. I conclude that Barreto has something significant to teach us about the complexities of humanization and the limits of critical education.

---

1   For examples of the first approach see Carr (2005), Gribble (1983), Jollimore and Barrios (2006), and Palmer (1992). For the second, see Roberts (2012, 2015), Roberts and Freeman-Moir (2013), Roberts and Saeverot (2018). In relation to Freire's work in particular, see Roberts (2010, ch. 7), Rozas Gomez (2013), and Vahl, Arriada, and Nogueira (2021).
2   On the political dimensions of the novel, see Bollig (2003), Corrêa (2017), Schwarcz (2014), Serra (2011), and Valente (2013). For a detailed examination of Policarpo's character, see Wasserman (1992).

Lima Barreto and *The Sad End of Policarpo Quaresma*

Afonso Henriques de Lima Barreto was born in Rio de Janeiro in 1881 and died in 1922.[3] His short life was marked by extremes: solidarity and alienation, hope and disillusionment, responsibility and recklessness. Both his parents had a strong commitment to education. His mother had come from a family of slaves but was, with the support of her parents, able to become a teacher; his father too had humble beginnings, but was later to find success as a typographer, gaining an appointment to the National Press (Serra, 2011, p. 30). Despite these achievements, the family struggled financially, and their circumstances became even more difficult when Barreto's mother died. He was just six years old at the time. Encouraged by his father, Barreto did well in school but approached his post-school studies with less enthusiasm. He did, however, retain a love of reading nurtured by his father, making regular visits to the National Library to peruse literary and philosophical texts. During his post-school years he developed enduring friendships but also, in the presence of other students who had come from more privileged Brazilian families, an acute and troubling 'awareness of his difference, of his class and his color' (p. 31).[4] His nascent interest in writing found expression in his pseudonymous portraits, 'often cutting and sarcastic,' of professors and students in a student magazine (p. 32).

When his father's mental health declined, responsibility for the family fell to Barreto. His failure to successfully complete the requirements to graduate as an engineer forced him to seek other employment, and he took up a clerical position with the War Ministry. The lack of stimulation in his daily working life found some compensation in the stability afforded by a steady income, and his talents as a writer began to flourish. He started to compose short stories and novels, while also building on his earlier journalistic efforts with contributions to newspapers and magazines. With his growing maturity as a writer, his personal, professional, and political preferences became clearer. Influenced by Dostoevsky's portrayal of the wretchedness of the human condition, and by Swift's satirizing of dysfunctional and corrupt institutions, Barreto came to see literature as 'a product of society and an instrument for elucidating the relationships that govern it, as well as a means of correcting its errors' (p. 32). His particular interest in 'the status of Afro-Brazilians, inhabitants of the suburbs and immigrants' provided fodder for his books (p. 32). Barreto was aware his criticisms of racism would not be well received in some

---

3 I am indebted to Serra (2011) for many of the biographical details provided in this section.
4 See also, Schwarcz (2017) and Wasserman (2008).

quarters (Schwarcz, 2014). He was adamant, however, that what was needed was 'a militant literature, for the greater glory of our species, on earth and even in heaven' (Serra, 2011, p. 33).

Barreto wrote *The Sad End of Policarpo Quaresma* at great speed, completing the manuscript – while still employed at the War Ministry – between January and March of 1911. The work initially appeared in instalments in the *Journal of Trade* (Serra, 2011, p. 37); it was not published in book form until 1915. Barreto had to finance the publication and promotion of the novel himself, borrowing money to do so. His resentment at finding himself in such a situation was compounded by the poor quality of the published work, which was littered with mistakes (Schwarcz, 2014). *The Sad End of Policarpo Quaresma* was written against a backdrop of social upheaval in Brazil. Slavery had been abolished and in 1889 the country had been declared a Republic. For Barreto, any hope that Brazilian independence would bring 'emancipatory change' quickly gave way to a realization that 'modernity and Republicanism served power much more than they subverted it' (Aidoo & Silva, 2013, p. 2). Aided by the military, the new regime adopted an authoritarian approach to governance. Protests and uprisings followed. In Rio de Janeiro, urban development brought some improvements but also led to the creation of slums as the poor were pushed out of the city center. Barreto's life too was in a state of change. The publication of *The Sad End of Policarpo Quaresma* marked a transition from one phase in his career to another: hitherto accepted and admired by many in literary and journalistic circles, he would experience a growing isolation from his peers (Schwarcz, 2014).

Barreto's persistent criticism of political, cultural and military life in Brazil was always bound to create tensions, and his alienation from others was exacerbated by his alcoholism. His father was by now a complete dependent and his psychiatric episodes undoubtedly put Barreto under further strain. The family moved twice but remained in the suburb of Todos os Santos (Serra, 2011, p. 37). Barreto's view of himself as a potential Nobel laureate did not stop him from attacking almost everyone and everything via his polemical articles: 'He derided those in power, diplomats, academics, politicians, capitalists, other writers' (p. 36). His behavior became increasingly erratic. He would sometimes leave groups of friends and later be found 'wandering the streets drunk, his clothes in tatters' (p. 39). Like his father before him, Barreto was committed to a psychiatric institution, first in 1914 and again in 1919. After several periods of sick leave, he finally retired, in 1918, from his position at the War Ministry. Remarkably, his productivity as a writer continued unabated during these years. In addition to his newspaper pieces, he worked on short stories, essays, and novels. He never quite achieved the literary recognition he so desperately sought, his three approaches to the Brazilian Academy of Letters all coming to nothing, and he was found dead in his home in November 1922, his father passing away two days later (pp. 40–41).

The Sad End of Policarpo Quaresma is structured in three parts. The first part introduces the reader to the central character, Policarpo Quaresma, an ordinary civil servant who lives a quiet life, his habits so regular people can tell the time just by watching him. Major Quaresma, as he is also known, has few friends but also no enemies. It is no secret that he has a large collection of books, but the Major keeps his reading preferences to himself. In the early chapters of the novel we also meet some of Policarpo's key acquaintances: his sister Adelaide (with whom he lives), General Albernaz and his family (including Olga, Policarpo's goddaughter), his servant Anastácio, and Ricardo, a local musician. The first hint that something unusual might disrupt the unobtrusive routine Policarpo has established over the last thirty years is his decision to take up guitar lessons with Ricardo. His sister, reflecting prevailing attitudes in the neighborhood, is aghast that a man of her brother's age and standing would want to learn such an inferior instrument and associate with a 'vulgar singer' such as Ricardo (Barreto, 2011, p. 51). Policarpo corrects her, noting that the modinha is 'the most authentic expression of Brazilian poetry and the guitar … the instrument it calls for!' (p. 51). Major Quaresma, it turns out, is a patriot, with a deep love, cultivated through decades of reading, of Brazil's customs and traditions as well as its natural beauty and bounty. This hitherto hidden passion finds further expression in Policarpo's subsequent words and actions. When receiving visitors one day, he suddenly starts crying and pulling at his hair, explaining to his bewildered guests that this was how Brazilians greeted each other in the past. He also petitions government officials to adopt the indigenous Tupi-Guaraní as Brazil's official language, a suggestion that is greeted with ridicule and contempt. He suffers a breakdown and is committed to an asylum on the Praia das Saudades.

The second part focuses on Policarpo's activities following his release, after six months, from psychiatric confinement. He has recovered some of his strength, and with his patriotic fervor intact, he throws himself into a new venture: farming. Taking early retirement from his clerical position, and at the prompting of his goddaughter, he moves to 'The Haven,' a small rural holding two hours by rail from Rio de Janeiro. Convinced that Brazilian soils are the best in the world, and informed by his reading of works on geology, zoology, and botany, he plans his garden meticulously. He prepares complicated inventories not just for plants but also for animals. With the help of Anastácio, he tends tirelessly to his land, weeding, hoeing the rough soil, and sowing seeds. He sees some progress, and is encouraged by this, feeling especially proud of the root vegetables he takes to market – the product of his sweat, his toil, having grown them from scratch. The fact that his expenses outweigh his modest earnings troubles his sister but does not bother the Major: he is in this game for reasons other than money. Policarpo is propelled by grandiose visions of his efforts leading to a duplication of similar initiatives in Brazil, dispensing with the need for European and Argentinean imports. But in the end his battles with nature, and particularly with the invasive ants that had plagued so many others before him, prove too much. His situation worsens with the intrusion of some unwelcome visitors, and having persisted with earnest intent for as long as possible, he is forced to abandon his agricultural ventures.

Part Three concentrates on Policarpo's involvement, as a volunteer, with the Brazilian military. At this point in the book, a real figure from Barreto's time – President Marshal Floriano Peixoto – enters the narrative. Initially supportive of the President, Policarpo comes to form an increasingly critical view of his moral character. Floriano is portrayed as a mediocre military strategist and a brutal tyrant, surrounded by auxiliaries equally lacking in integrity, intelligence, and commitment. Policarpo attempts to appeal to the leader's reason, preparing a report with proposals for the social and economic advancement of Brazil. Floriano, when asked by the Major about the legislative reforms he (Policarpo) has proposed, is dismissive but controlled in his response. Carried away by the enthusiasm he has for his ideals, Quaresma fails to notice a 'dangerous irritation' in the dictator's countenance. 'You, Quaresma, are a visionary …,' Floriano declares (p. 347), later events proving that the term was not intended as a compliment. Policarpo is wounded, but not too seriously. He is released from hospital and is assigned the uncomfortable role of jailor. His horror at the way prisoners are treated is not shared by others in more powerful positions. His compassion and conscience lead to his ultimate downfall. He is arrested, without knowing what charges have been laid against him. He suspects, however, that they relate to a letter he had sent to Floriano protesting the slaughter of a 'group of wretches, chosen at random' (p. 407). He reflects on the failures in his life, admitting to himself that his endeavors have not brought him happiness (p. 408). Ricardo and Olga try desperately to save him, but their pleas fall on deaf ears. Quaresma is labeled a lunatic, an outlaw, and a traitor. As the novel closes, his fate seems to be sealed and Olga is left to wonder whether it might be better to let him die, 'heroically and alone on some island in the bay, taking his honour, his kindness, his moral character untarnished to the grave' (p. 423).

Conscientization, Compassion, and Madness: Freire and Barreto

As noted in earlier chapters, Paulo Freire's ideas have frequently been compared with those of other writers.[5] To date, however, there has been little attention to connections between his thought and the work of Lima Barreto.[6] In some respects, the prospects for a fruitful comparison between these two important Brazilian figures might not seem promising. Freire and Barreto engaged in their own distinct forms of writing, for their own reasons. Barreto's contributions were literary, journalisticy, and polemical; Freire authored scholarly works. Their lives barely overlapped (Freire was born the year prior to Barreto's death), and by the time Freire published his first book in the late 1960s, Brazil and the wider world had changed considerably. Barreto lived through World War One but did not witness the horrors that were to follow with the rise of Nazism and World War Two. Urban centers in Brazil continued to grow and develop, and there was further political upheaval, culminating in a military coup in 1964. Barreto's main source of income for much of his adulthood was his clerical position; Freire was employed in social service and educational roles. The two men also appear to have differed quite substantially in their temperaments, Barreto's irascible and erratic character contrasting with Freire's more congenial, stable personality. Barreto's battles with alcohol and psychiatric illness find no parallel in Freire's biography. Barreto had barely reached middle age when he died; Freire enjoyed several further decades of life.

In probing further, however, some interesting points in common can be identified. Both Barreto and Freire suffered a degree of hardship in their formative years. The period following the loss of his mother was especially difficult for Barreto, and Freire's family struggled during the years of the Great Depression. Freire also endured the pain of losing a parent (his father) at a young age. Freire may not have had the same self-destructive tendencies as Barreto, but he did come to regret his long-time smoking habit. Neither Freire nor Barreto were cold, detached rationalists; both were passionate, energetic, committed individuals. Both were fearless in their critique of oppressive systems, structures, and ideas. Barreto's whole career was shaped by the deep racial inequalities that characterized the Brazil of his time; Freire was heavily involved with impoverished communities,

---

5   For a comprehensive discussion of some of the comparisons that have been made, see Schugurensky (2011).
6   An exception, in the Portuguese language, is da Silva (2014). At the time of writing, few, if any, studies appear to have been published in English.

in both rural and urban environments. Both experienced marginalization, Freire through enforced exile, Barreto while remaining in Brazil. Neither pretended to be 'neutral' in their stance as writers; both believed that writing could, and should, play a part in addressing wider social concerns. Freire and Barreto shared a love of reading and books, from a young age, and they also set high standards for themselves in their own writing. They sought to communicate directly, clearly and honestly, and tried to remain true to their ideals even when it would have been easier to do otherwise. Barreto addressed a remarkably diverse range of topics in his writing; Freire, too, ranged widely over a number of different themes in his work. Education was pivotal in the lives of both men, most obviously so for Freire but also for Barreto in the expectations nurtured by his parents. Barreto and Freire both worked extremely hard, remaining productive as writers during some of the most turbulent and demanding periods of their lives.

What might we say about *The Sad End of Policarpo Quaresma* from a Freirean point of view? And what, in turn, does the book have to 'say' to Freirean theory? In answering these questions, attention must be paid to both the political and historical backdrop that frames Barreto's narrative and the characters that populate the book. There is much in the picture of Brazil painted by Barreto that is, in Freirean terms, utterly dehumanizing. Humanization, it is worth repeating, lies at the heart of Freire's philosophy of education.[7] We humanize ourselves, Freire (1972a) argues, through critical, dialogical, transformative praxis. Humanization is not merely a form of self-development; it also has to do with our relationships with others. If we are committed to the ideal of humanization, our starting point in meeting a fellow human being will be to see him or her as someone who 'thinks, is sensitive and has wisdom to share' (Arriada et al., 2019, p. 4). Structures, actions, and attitudes that impede the pursuit of humanization are dehumanizing. Such impediments are evident at multiple levels in *The Sad End of Policarpo Quaresma*. The book shows sexism, racism, and classism at work, sometimes forcefully, sometimes in more subtle ways. The Brazil depicted in Barreto's story is divisive and hierarchical. Barreto's narrator paints an unflattering portrait of Brazil's political and military leadership in the latter part of the 19th century, and shines a critical light on the bureaucratic and legal systems of the country at the time. *The Sad End of Policarpo Quaresma* also demonstrates the devastating consequences of closed-mindedness and unreflective acceptance of established customs and beliefs. It depicts a certain kind of *blindness* that is evident not merely in individuals but also at a systemic level. There is madness in the labyrinthine world of bureaucracy,

---

7 On Freire's approach to humanization, see Kirylo (2011), Mayo (1999), Morrow and Torres (2002), Roberts (2000), and Schugurensky (2011).

in many of the institutions we inhabit, and in the patterns of consumption that structure our lives. What appears 'natural' or 'normal' in one epoch will often be regarded as abhorrent at a later time in world history. Policarpo Quaresma is the character who goes 'mad' in this book, but Barreto also encourages us to question that madness and to open our eyes to other forms of insanity all around us.

Policarpo Quaresma shares much in common with Cervantes' (2005) extraordinary literary creation, Don Quixote. Both are tragi-comic figures who inhabit a world of their own. Others look on at them with curiosity, amusement, and concern. They are subject to scorn and ridicule but also to acts of genuine kindness and care. Both are utterly dedicated to their ideals: in Don Quixote's case, the vocation of knight errantry; for Policarpo, the upholding of Brazilian traditions and customs. They have a sincerity that is lacking in many with whom they come into contact. There is a coherence between the ideals they espouse and the way they try to live their lives. Don Quixote's friendship with his faithful squire Sancho Panza forms an important part of his tale, the latter growing as a character and shaping, as well as being shaped by, his Master (cf. Dienstag, 2006). Policarpo too has his supporters, though they do not follow him on his quest. The narrator's voice in both *Don Quixote* and *The Sad End of Policarpo Quaresma* is quiet but sympathetic, allowing the reader sufficient space to develop his or her own distinctive relationship with the central character of each work. The reader is given ample opportunity to ponder the nature of the 'madness' that inflicts both characters, and to reflect, in turn, on what might reasonably be regarded as sane and reasonable. In Cervantes' great novel, composed in two parts,[8] Don Quixote eventually returns to his home and dies peacefully; in Barreto's masterwork, the ending is ominous but not decisive. The two works are separated by four centuries, but they are linked by the ethical and educational problems they raise, and remain as relevant today as they were 100 or 400 years ago.

Freire has very little to say, directly, about 'madness.' This is hardly surprising, given the focus of his professional life. He was an educationist, not a psychiatrist, psychologist, or counselor. That said, there is, in his early books in particular, an implicit acknowledgment of the potential value of work in these fields in understanding the complexities of oppression and liberation. In *Pedagogy of the Oppressed* (Freire, 1972a) and *Cultural Action for Freedom* (Freire, 1972b), Freire makes reference to a number of thinkers with backgrounds in one or more of these areas, including Erich Fromm, Franz Fanon, and Herbert Marcuse. This influence can also be detected, from time to time, in later works. In *Pedagogy of Hope*,

---

8 The second part was written a decade after the first, following the release of a 'false' Quixote sequel by a literary imposter.

for instance, Freire (1994) maintains that a dialectical approach is necessary if we are to comprehend 'the phenomenon of the introjection of the oppressor by the oppressed, the latter's "adherence" to the former, the difficulty that the oppressed have in localizing the oppressor outside themselves' (p. 105). In reflecting on these ideas, as essential elements in his theory of education as conscientization, he recalls a conversation with Fromm, who noted: 'An educational practice like that is a kind of historico-sociocultural and political psychoanalysis' (p. 105). There is, it might be said, a kind of suppressed depth psychology at work in Freire's philosophy and pedagogy, that remains underdeveloped but warrants further exploration. An agenda for inquiry in this direction might include a range of possible empirical as well as theoretical paths for investigation. Outlining such an agenda is, however, beyond the scope of the present discussion. It must suffice here to note that interesting psychological, ethical, and educational questions arise when characters such as Don Quixote and Policarpo Quaresma (or their equivalents in 'real life') are considered in the light of Freire's ideas. Freire would, it seems clear, want to encourage us to adopt a compassionate stance when encountering characters of this kind. 'Compassion' in this context does not mean 'pity'; rather, it implies a genuine attempt to understand others. It requires a willingness to listen and to learn, with humility, openness, and love. Compassion demands care and commitment. These qualities are, as the discussion below suggests, all important elements of Freire's ethic.[9] There is much in Freire's philosophy that is helpful in enabling readers to form a thoughtful, sensitive, attentive relationship with a fictional character like Policarpo Quaresma. But this relationship is, as it were, two-way: Policarpo also 'speaks back' to Freire, posing some searching questions in relation to his ideal of humanizing education.

Freirean educational theory places particular emphasis on the development of a critical orientation toward the world. In Freire's earlier work (Freire, 1972b, 1976), this principle was developed via the concept of conscientization. In reflecting on patterns of thought and forms of life among his fellow Brazilians, Freire identified three broad modes of consciousness: magical, naïve, and critical. Magical consciousness was, he argued, most prominent among poor peasant communities. Those who exhibited this way of thinking were fatalistic in their outlook; they tended to attribute social and personal difficulties to destiny or God's will. They acted, for the most part, in accordance with tradition and custom, seldom questioning received wisdom. Their focus was mainly on meeting the basic physical needs of daily life. They lived in a kind of permanent 'today,' and were encouraged to do so by those (e.g., their landlords) who had an interest in maintaining an

---

9 See also Barros (2020, p. 161) on conscientization and 'embodied compassion.'

unequal social order. The emergence of a 'naïve' consciousness coincided with the development of a new urban class in Brazil. Here there was a focus on reform but a lack of interest in substantial structural change. Individualism and an ethic of self-advancement prevailed over collective action, and rhetoric ruled over rigor. Critical consciousness was not linked to any existing groups or given period in Brazil's history, but was favored by Freire, and is characterized by depth and perceptiveness in the identification, interpretation, and analysis of problems. A commitment to dialogue, an openness to the new without an unreflective rejection of the old, and a willingness to act on well-informed convictions are other features of this mode of consciousness.

Policarpo Quaresma does not fit neatly into any one of the three categories identified by Freire. In some of his pronouncements and plans there is an adherence to tradition that is characteristic of magical consciousness, but he is not fatalistic. He does not see his own problems, or those experienced by other Brazilians, as 'God's will' or as an inevitable fate that cannot be altered. He exhibits some resistance to the 'new,' and his embrace of the 'old' seems, at first glance, to be unbalanced and obsessive. He is passionate in his quest to revive ancient Brazilian customs. While his actions seem at times to be bizarre, some of his proposals – notably, the recommendation that an indigenous language be recognized and respected through official use – are far-reaching in their cultural, social, and political implications, and well ahead of their time. The economic principle he embraces of making the most of national and local resources, rather than relying on imports from elsewhere in the world, is similarly far-sighted. Major Quaresma wants to see change in Brazil, of both a 'reformist' and a 'radical' kind. He seeks to engage in dialogue with others – including the Brazilian President – but his efforts in this direction are largely ignored. Few take the time to truly listen to what he has to say. Policarpo himself lacks openness in some respects, but so do many of the people with whom he comes into contact. The changes he proposes, while looking back, also look forward and would, if taken seriously, require substantial shifts in Brazil's economic and legal systems. Where he senses injustice, he is willing to act on his convictions, placing himself at considerable risk in doing so. His quest is, in one sense, merely the idiosyncratic endeavor of a single individual, yet there is also a collective dimension to the changes implied by his proposals. Policarpo Quaresma is, in short, a complex, sometimes contradictory, mix of different attributes and qualities. He is not merely 'magical' nor 'naïve' in his thinking, though elements of those modes of consciousness are evident, and while some of his words, attitudes and deeds are consistent with the ideal of critical consciousness, others are not.

Freire, it must be stressed, did not intend the categories of magical, naïve, and critical consciousness to be seen as fixed, universal 'stages' of individual development. His concern, at least in the case of magical and naïve modes of consciousness, was with specific groups, at given moments in Brazil's history. His use of these categories was limited mainly to his early publications, and it is important to place these ideas in the broader context of his work as a whole.[10] Even so, Policarpo constitutes a fascinating case study, when considered in relation to Freire's ethical and educational preferences. His exhibits many of the qualities that are often seen as typical of an educated person. He has read widely, over many decades, and reflected carefully on the society in which he lives. He demonstrates both breadth and depth in his knowledge of Brazilian customs. He can speak and write eloquently when discussing his interests. And yet, there is also something slightly out of kilter in his character, his countenance, and his actions. For all his knowledge, he lacks a certain sense of balance and perspective in his understanding of himself, others, and the world. It is not a form of self-obsessiveness that is at work here; indeed, he pays relatively little attention to himself. His focus is more on his country and its cultural health than his own welfare. That is part of the problem; he cannot see himself as others do, and this leaves him vulnerable to a variety of dehumanizing responses – from condescension to manipulation and persecution. He is unable to fully 'connect' with others when trying to convey his ideas to them. The fault in such situations undoubtedly rests not just with him but also with those he encounters in his social relationships; they fail in their ethical duty to pay proper attention to him.[11] But Policarpo also does not always help himself in such situations. His devotion to a romanticized view of Brazilian life prevents him from detecting some of the crucial nuances in human interactions and from finding an effective way to engage others in a dialogue with him.

Barreto, like Cervantes, seems to suggest that reading, of a particular kind, can be harmful. Cervantes makes it clear that Don Quixote has spent too much time immersed in tales of chivalry, and this preoccupation has distorted his perception of reality. Barreto shows that Policarpo's decades of reading, in private, have similarly contributed to the creation of a kind of alternative patriotic world for Major Quaresma. In Freirean terms, neither Don Quixote nor Policarpo Quaresma read in an authentically critical manner. For Freire, critical reading involves placing texts in their broader social, political, cultural, and economic contexts. A reader, he argues, should both challenge and be challenged by what he or she is reading.

---

10 See further, Liu (2014) and Roberts (2000).
11 This point is made with the work of Simone Weil in mind. For Weil, the cultivation of our capacity for attention is a key epistemological, ethical and educational task (see Catton, 2019; Roberts, 2016; Weil, 1997, 2001). For a cautionary note on how attention can be 'economized,' see Reveley (2015).

A critical posture implies neither passivity nor aggression. Patience and persistence are necessary if one is to read well. Freire spoke at times of the need to read a book through once, and then to read it again, the second time with a sharper critical eye. Critical readers ask questions of the texts they encounter, but they also allow an author's words to pose questions for them. Reading in this manner carries the risk of having one's view of the world, or at least some aspects of that worldview, overturned. Reading, as Freire saw it, should be a dialogical process. In cases where an individual sits down with a book, reading may appear to be a solitary activity, but even under those circumstances the reader is never 'alone.' From a Freirean point of view, a reader can enter into a purposeful, thoughtful 'conversation' with the author of a book. That author will, in turn, have been shaped in his or her thinking by his or her relations with others. Freire wanted readers to not only contextualize the work of the authors they read but also to draw connections between the author's ideas and their own contexts. Readers can often make insightful links between the themes addressed in a text and the problems and possibilities that exist for them and/or for others in their time and place. There should, Freire believed, be a linking of 'word' with 'world.' Reading has a role to play in facilitating relaxation but the kind of reading that mattered most for Freire is demanding and difficult. Reading can be unsettling and troubling, but constructively so. Critical reading is transformative; it shakes us up and prompts us to action. Reading, from a Freirean perspective, should deepen our understanding of ourselves and the world and, in so doing, play its part in the broader process of humanization.[12]

Policarpo Quaresma's reading habits seem to fall short of the critical ideal Freire espouses. We learn that the Major has a large collection of books and that he has read widely. But he has not learned how to adequately contextualize what he reads. He longs for a past that never existed, for a Brazil that was more fertile, more inventive and industrious, more beautiful than could ever have been the case. He builds up an idealized picture in mind, lulling himself into a form of sleep in examining both the past and the present. Freire (1972a) counsels us to have faith in our fellow human beings, but Policarpo's faith in others is arguably misplaced. Lacking the ability to read subtle cues in social situations, he naively expects others to share his own view of the world. His blind commitment to an impossible ideal can be tolerated when it remains a private affair. But once Policarpo steps away from his bookcase into the thoroughly imperfect world of Brazilian politics, the brutality of that world is thrown into sharp relief. The Major is bewildered when others do not operate in a reasonable manner; he cannot understand why his

---

12 See further, Freire (1985, 1996), Freire and Macedo (1987), Freire and Shor (1987), and Roberts (2000, 2010).

petitioning, his references to the findings of his private research, his arguments, fall on deaf ears. His naïve faith in the power of reason leads, with a certain irony, to his loss of reason; he enters the mysterious world of madness, and his alienation from others becomes even more entrenched. Policarpo is propelled into action by the cumulative effect of decades of reading, but he does not ask sufficiently searching questions of his books, or of himself. His example shows that more is not always better in reading. Breadth in reading is not always accompanied by breadth in understanding. For Policarpo, wide reading actually leads to a narrowing of his sphere of vision. The Major may have a mind full of ideas from his books, and his knowledge of Brazilian history is impressive, but his ability to harness insights from his reading to see clearly what is right in front of him is sometimes limited.

Of significance in considering the case of Policarpo Quaresma is the question of his education. His reading, it has already been noted, has for most of his life been conducted in private. He learns a great deal from all the books he reads over the years, but he has not, as far as we can gather, been *taught* how to read (as an adult). This highlights a crucial point in Freirean theory: teachers have a vital role to play in guiding others. Freire's critique of banking education in his early work (Freire, 1972a) led some to believe that he was somehow 'against' teachers or teaching. This was a profound misreading of his intentions, as he made clear on numerous occasions in subsequent years.[13] He insisted that he was a teacher and not merely a facilitator. He was against authoritarianism in education but not against the appropriate exercising of authority. Authority is evident in the knowledge the teacher has, or should have, of his or her subject. It is also apparent in the pedagogical decisions made in educational settings. Teaching and learning in institutions such as schools and universities should not, from a Freirean standpoint, proceed on an 'anything goes' basis. Freire stressed the need for a clear sense of direction in education, and teachers have a responsibility to help in providing this. Dialogue in Freirean education is not idle chatter; it should, to the contrary, be structured, purposeful and rigorous (Freire & Shor, 1987; Roberts, 2000). All of this is lacking in Policarpo's learning environment. In deciding to learn how to play the guitar, Policarpo turns to a Master of the art as his guide. In reading his books, however, he is untutored. He only 'tries out' his ideas with others after a long period – stretching over not just months or years but decades – of reading and interpreting and reflecting on his own. He has not learned how to engage in the constructive cut and thrust of educational dialogue. He has received no guidance from a teacher who has already developed an intimate, in-depth, sophisticated

---

13 See, for example, Freire (1987, 1997a, 1998a), Freire and Macedo (1995), Freire and Shor (1987), and Horton and Freire (1990).

knowledge of the texts he is reading. By the time he is ready to take his plans to the world, he is too fervently committed to his ideas to contemplate the possibility of examining them critically; he leaves himself exposed, in an educational sense, to dangers he is ill-prepared to meet.

There is a particularly moving section in Barreto's novel where the narrator reflects on Policarpo and his fellow 'inmates' at the psychiatric institution in Praia das Saudades (Barreto, 2011, pp. 172–173). All of the residents at the institution have their own peculiarities. Some who are poor say they are rich, and vice versa. There are scholars who curse scholarship. There is a man who calls himself 'Attila' and claims to have killed many people. After six months there, the Major is calmer but his attitude is more one of resignation than rejuvenation. In his outward manner, he appears to be a 'normal' man, but it is uncertain whether he has been 'cured.' He may no longer be classified as 'mad,' but he retains the dream he has nurtured for so long. His six months in the institution have 'served more for rest and seclusion than for psychiatric therapy' (p. 172). Quaresma leaves, 'sadder than he had ever been' (p. 173). 'Of all the sad things to see in this world,' the narrator muses, 'the saddest is madness; it is the bleakest and the most heart-rending' (p. 173). The text continues:

> Our lives carry on as normal, but this imperceptible yet profound and almost always unfathomable disturbance renders them entirely useless. It appears to stem from something that is stronger than we are, goading us on, in whose hands we are no more than puppets. There were cultures in the past that regarded madness as sacred; perhaps this is the explanation why, when we hear a madman raving, we are overcome by a sensation that he is not the one who is speaking – It is someone else, seeing for him, interpreting for him, someone who is there behind him, invisible! ... (p. 173)

This beautiful passage raises some interesting questions in relation to Freirean theory. What would we say, from a Freirean point of view, about someone who exhibits the characteristics of madness, as depicted above? A person who is 'mad' in the sense described by Barreto's narrator could not be seen as critically conscious in Freirean terms; nor could he or she be classified as merely 'naïve.' The inner state portrayed in the quoted passage has a certain 'magical' quality to it, but it is of a different order to the magical consciousness Freire identified among peasant communities in Brazil. Cases of the kind being considered here also pose problems for Freire's account of humanization. Are those who are 'mad' dehumanized by their madness? How, if at all, might they humanize themselves? Freire's ethic does not provide clear answers to these questions. If humanization means engaging in critical, dialogical praxis, what are we to say when the possibilities for being both critical and dialogical, as Freire understands those terms, are severely compromised or eliminated by a psychiatric condition? In what ways, if at all, might those in such a state 'transform' themselves, and the world, through reflection and action?

The Freirean principle of always contextualizing is important here. We need, when considering questions of the kind raised above, to examine the particulars of given cases. Each individual in a psychiatric institution, or anywhere else, will have his or her own distinctive strengths and weaknesses, and circumstances, that must be understood when considering possibilities for education and humanization. While the use of a broad label such as 'madness' might have been acceptable in Barreto's time, today individuals tend to be diagnosed in more nuanced ways, with care plans that vary accordingly.[14] There is now an extensive body of research, on a host of different psychiatric conditions, from which health professionals and others can draw in deciding on effective treatments once diagnoses have been made. Care will often be provided not just in institutions but in communities, with a range of support structures in place. In many countries, governments have made an effort to reduce the stigma that has sometimes been attached to mental illness in the past. Laws are now in place to better protect the rights of those who are most vulnerable. In short, much has changed since the time at which *The Sad End of Policarpo Quaresma* was written. Nevertheless, there remains something deeply unsettling in the observations made by Barreto's narrator, and the discomfort experienced by readers in accompanying Major Quaresma on his journey is worthy of continuing reflection from an educational and ethical point of view.

In some respects, the questions raised by Barreto's novel go beyond the idea of 'madness,' or any of its more nuanced contemporary equivalents, conceived in purely clinical terms. *The Sad End of Policarpo Quaresma* points to the bewildering and often dispiriting impasse that can sometimes be reached, but not crossed, in educational communication. There is something at stake here, of ethical and educative importance, that cannot be adequately captured by the notion of a psychiatric condition. There is a certain incommensurability in worldviews, in modes of thinking, feeling and being, that can emerge in clinical settings, and in educational programs, where the ideal of dialogue appears to break down. The sadness to which the narrator refers might be explained, in part, by the sense of loss we experience when prospects for communication are seriously impeded. Freire argues that we are social beings: we exist in and with the world not as isolated individuals but through our relationships with others.[15] This idea is evident in Freire's epistemology, his

---

14   For one influential account of the history of 'madness,' see Foucault (2001).
15   This position is not inconsistent with the existentialist view, taken from Kierkegaard (2009), that each individual is utterly unique, with his or her own distinctive circumstances, relationships, struggles, hopes, abilities, commitments, and dreams (see further, Webster, 2016).

ethic, and his pedagogy. When there appears to be no way through to other people, no way of establishing a human connection with them, a sense of tragic loss can emerge. The loss here is both for the one wanting to make that human connection and for the one with whom it cannot be made. If, as Barreto's narrator implies, the person afflicted with madness appears to be 'possessed' by some force beyond him- or herself, we may grieve his or her loss of any meaningful form of human control. A person who suffers in this way cannot be said to exercise autonomy or experience freedom, in a manner consistent with Freire's ethical ideal, and this renders the task of education in such situations problematic (cf. Petrovic & Rolstad, 2016). Freire's approach to education is premised on the idea that participants in a pedagogical situation are treated as thinking, feeling *subjects*, not as objects to be manipulated, indoctrinated, or ignored. It is this denial of subjectivity, via authoritarian pedagogical practices and relationships, as part of wider oppressive social system, that constitutes the heart of what Freire refers to as banking education (Freire, 1972a). Freire's favoring of problem-posing education over banking education presupposes the ability to pose problems and ask questions, in a critically self-aware manner, with others who are also committed to learning, under the guidance of a well-prepared teacher (cf. Beckett, 2013; Jackson, 2016). Freedom, for Freire, is not the same as license. In a pedagogical setting, it is freedom with limits – limits structured by the purposeful, respectful, reflective participation of human subjects in a dialogical educative process.

Freire does provide a helpful starting point for educational encounters, under any circumstances, in the emphasis he places on the virtue of *love* (Darder, 2002; Fraser, 1997). This, for him, is one of the keys to any worthwhile educational relationship. Teachers should, he maintains, have a love of their subject areas and a passion for study, but they should also love the students with whom they work. It is, of course, not romantic love that he has in mind here, but love as a form of care and commitment.[16] We should, if we are committed to our task as educators, want to do all we can to draw out the best from the students we teach. Love comes from recognizing that we are all engaged in a process of struggle to make sense of ourselves and the world. Love is built on a platform of humility: the humility to recognize that there is much that we do not know, and that we are all flawed, necessarily incomplete beings. It is perhaps precisely in situations where communication is most difficult, where the work required to establish a human connection seems unending or fruitless, that pedagogical love of the kind favored by Freire is most

---

16   This resonates with the ideal of attentive love found developed by Iris Murdoch (see Delaune, 2020; McMenamin, 2017; Murdoch, 2001; Roberts & Freeman-Moir, 2013, ch. 3; Roberts & Saeverot, 2018, ch. 2).

necessary. There are risks in such encounters, to be sure. Compassion, if it is not exercised with care, can become patronizing or presumptuous. Working with those who seem most distant from us can be extraordinarily stressful and draining. Yet, these dangers need to deter us from taking action. Patience and persistence, both partners with humility, will be needed in such situations. Honesty and integrity in examining our own preferences, prejudices, and weaknesses will also be required. Freire does not provide a neat set of rules for negotiating such situations. His educational philosophy does, however, suggest some underlying principles that can be adapted and applied by teachers in a variety of different pedagogical settings, with students of all ages and abilities.[17]

Every pedagogical encounter places its own distinctive demands on us, and there may be cases where, as teachers, we feel that we simply do not know what to do. Freire was sensitive to such possibilities.[18] Getting away from the mentality that there will always be a 'solution' to the pedagogical problems we encounter can be crucial. Freire reminds us that the uncertainties we experience as teachers are not merely tolerable but essential to the educational process. Doubt can be debilitating but it can, as argued in Chapter Two of this book, also be enabling; it can provide just the spark we need to keep thinking, keep observing, keep talking with others, and in so doing, make educational progress. This process is necessarily incomplete, for as one problem in an educational setting is addressed, new problems arise. We need not feel threatened by this never-ending cycle; instead, Freire might say, we can find it invigorating. Education implies movement. It can bring suffering and even despair, as well as profound happiness.[19] It is meant to challenge us and may make us feel uncomfortable. Education involves a process of inner struggle; it does not allow us to ever fully and finally 'sit still.' A commitment to education requires of us that we accept a certain restlessness as a permanent feature of our lives. In *The Sad End of Policarpo Quaresma*, Lima Barreto leaves us with a sense of uneasiness – not just over the fate of the Major but also over *ourselves*. Policarpo may have gone 'mad,' but his fragilities as a human being are not too far removed from our own – from the struggles we all undergo, through our educational experiences, as we try to build meaningful lives.

17 See Freire, Fraser, Macedo, McKinnon, and Stokes (1997), Kirylo (2020), Peters and Besley (2015), Roberts (1999b), Shor (1987), and Torres (2019).
18 Freire's nuanced consideration of uncertainty in pedagogical situations is evident in these sources, among others: Freire (1994, 1997b, 1998a, b). On the uniqueness of every pedagogical encounter, see Saevi (2011).
19 See further, Carusi (2017), Chen (2016), Cigman (2014), Gibbs (2015), Gibbs and Dean (2014), Guilherme and de Freitas (2017), Jackson and Bingham (2018), Roberts (2016), Webster (2009), and Zembylas (2020).

Conclusion

Lima Barreto led a troubled life but this did not stop him from producing some remarkable work as a writer. The challenges he had to face in dealing with his mother's death, his father's descent into madness, and his first-hand experience of racism shaped his writing priorities and style. There is no one best way to read *The Sad End of Policarpo Quaresma*, but the approach taken here, focusing on the educative and ethical dilemmas posed by Barreto's central character, opens up further possibilities for worthwhile inquiry. There is more work that could be done in investigating the prospects for critical education among those who would, in Barreto's time, have been deemed 'mad.' If this task is taken seriously, lines between what is 'rational' and what is 'irrational' may end up being blurred. The point made by Barreto's narrator about madness being regarded in some cultures as sacred hints at what might be at stake in work of this kind. It is not just the person labeled as 'mad' who has something to learn. Those who inhabit inner worlds very different from our own can sometimes startle us with sudden insights, seemingly generated from nowhere, and prompt us to reconsider our pedagogical assumptions. Openness is necessary if we are to watch, wait, listen, and learn. It is not so much reverence for the mysterious other that must be cultivated as *respect* – respect for a fellow human being who plays his or her part in making us what we are. Freirean theory allows us to make some headway, as compassionate readers, in understanding Policarpo Quaresma, but it does not provide all the answers. Freire devoted most of his adult life to education, but right up to the moment of his death, he remained curious, ever ready to keep deepening and extending his understanding of himself, others, and the world. *The Sad End of Policarpo Quaresma* has something distinctive and valuable to offer all who share a similar zest for life and learning, and lends itself well to ongoing pedagogical reflection.

References

Aidoo, L., & Silva, D. F. (2013). Introduction. In L. Aidoo & D. F. Silva (Eds.), *Lima Barreto: New critical perspectives* (pp. 1–7). Lanham, MD: Lexington Books.
Aronowitz, S. (1993). Paulo Freire's radical democratic humanism. In P. McLaren & P. Leonard (Eds.), *Paulo Freire: A critical encounter* (pp. 8–24). London: Routledge.
Arriada, E., Nogueira, G. M., Vahl, M., & Zasso, S. M. B. (2019). *Pedagogy of the oppressed*: From the manuscript to the printed text. Revised version of a paper originally published in Portuguese in *Revista de Alfabetização Brasileira*.
Barreto, L. (2011). *Triste fim de Policarpo Quaresma/The sad end of Policarpo Quaresma* (M. Carlyon, Trans.). Rio de Janeiro: Instituto Cultural Cidade Viva.
Barros, S. (2020). Paulo Freire in a hall of mirrors. *Educational Theory, 70*(2), 151–169.
Beckett, D. (2008). Holistic competence: Putting judgements first. *Asia Pacific Education Review, 9*(1), 21–30.
Beckett, K. S. (2013). Paulo Freire and the concept of education. *Educational Philosophy and Theory, 45*(1), 49–62.
Beckett, K. (2018). John Dewey's conception of education: Finding common ground with R.S. Peters and Paulo Freire. *Educational Philosophy and Theory, 50*(4), 380–389.
Bee, B. (1980). The politics of literacy. In R. Mackie (Ed.), *Literacy and revolution: The pedagogy of Paulo Freire* (pp. 39–56). London: Pluto Press.
Benade, L. (2012). *From technicians to teachers: Ethical teaching in the context of globalized education reform*. New York: Continuum.

Benade, L. (2015). Bits, bytes and dinosaurs: Using Levinas and Freire to address the concept of 'twenty-first century learning'. *Educational Philosophy and Theory, 47*(9), 935–948.

Berger, P. (1974). *Pyramids of sacrifice: Political ethics and social change*. New York: Basic Books.

Berthold, D. (2011). *The ethics of authorship: Communication, seduction, and death in Hegel and Kierkegaard*. New York: Fordham University Press.

Biesta, G. J. J. (2014). *The beautiful risk of education*. Boulder, CO: Paradigm Publishers.

Bingham, C. (2016). Against educational humanism: Rethinking spectatorship in Dewey and Freire. *Studies in Philosophy and Education, 35*, 181–193.

Bojesen, E. (2018). Passive education. *Educational Philosophy and Theory, 50*(10), 928–935.

Bollig, B. (2003). *Triste fim de Policarpo Quaresma*, or the sad end of party politics in Belle Époque Brazil. *Hispanic Research Journal, 4*(1), 59–71.

Borg, C., & Mayo, P. (2000). Reflections from a "Third Age" marriage: Paulo Freire's pedagogy of reason, hope and passion – An interview with Ana Maria (Nita) Freire. *McGill Journal of Education, 35*(2), 105–120.

Bowers, C. A. (1983). Linguistic roots of cultural invasion in Paulo Freire's pedagogy. *Teachers College Record, 84*(4), 935–953.

Brady, A. (2017). Exile and inclusion: Excerpts from Albert Camus' *Exile and the Kingdom*. In P. Standish & N. Saito (Eds.), *The anxiety of inclusion*. Kyoto: Kyoto University Press.

Bronner, S. E. (1999). *Camus: Portrait of a moralist*. Chicago, IL: The University of Chicago Press.

Burch, K. (1999). Eros as the educational principle of democracy. *Studies in Philosophy and Education, 18*(3), 123–142.

Burgh, G., & Thornton, S. (2016). Inoculation against wonder: Finding an antidote in Camus, pragmatism and the community of inquiry. *Educational Philosophy and Theory, 48*(9), 884–898.

Byrne, C. (2011). Freirean critical pedagogy's challenge to interfaith education: What is interfaith? What is education? *British Journal of Religious Education, 33*(1), 47–60.

Camus, A. (1958). *Caligula and three other plays* (S. Gilbert, Trans.). New York: Vintage Books.

Camus, A. (1960). *The plague* (S. Gilbert, Trans.). London: Penguin.

Camus, A. (1968). *Lyrical and critical essays* (E. C. Kennedy, Trans.). New York: Vintage Books.

Camus, A. (1989). *The stranger* (M. Ward, Trans.). New York: Vintage.

Camus, A. (1991a). *Exile and the kingdom* (J. O'Brien, Trans.). New York: Vintage International.

Camus, A. (1991b). *The myth of Sisyphus and other essays* (J. O'Brien, Trans.). New York: Vintage International.

Camus, A. (1991c). *The rebel* (A. Bower, Trans.). New York: Vintage International.

Camus, A. (1995). *Resistance, rebellion, and death* (J. O'Brien, Trans.). New York: Vintage International.

Camus, A. (1996). *The first man* (D. Hapgood, Trans.). London: Penguin.

Camus, A. (2000). *The fall* (J. O'Brien, Trans.). London: Penguin.

Carr, D. (2005). On the contribution of literature and the arts to the educational cultivation of moral virtue, feeling and emotion. *Journal of Moral Education, 34*, 137–151.

Carreño, J. (2007). The imperfect metaphor of passion in Kierkegaard's *Philosophical Fragments*. *Tijdschrift voor Filosofie, 69*(3), 475–507.

Carusi, F. T. (2017). Why bother teaching? Despairing the ethical through teaching that does not follow. *Studies in Philosophy and Education, 36*, 633–645.

Catton, J. (2019). *Attention, literature and education*. PhD thesis, University of Canterbury, New Zealand.

Cervantes, M. de (2005). *Don Quixote* (E. Grossman, Trans.). London: Vintage.

Chambers, D. W. (2019). Is Freire incoherent? Reconciling directiveness and dialogue in Freirean pedagogy. *Journal of Philosophy of Education, 53*(1), 21–47.

Chen, R. H. (2011). Bearing and transcending suffering with nature and the world: A humanistic account. *Journal of Moral Education, 40*(2), 203–216.

Chen, R. H. (2016). Freire and a pedagogy of suffering: A moral ontology. In M. A. Peters (Ed.), *Encyclopedia of educational philosophy and theory*. Singapore: Springer.

Cigman, R. (2014). Happiness rich and poor: Lessons from philosophy and literature. *Journal of Philosophy of Education, 48*(2), 308–322.

Cockayne, J. (2015). Empathy and divine union in Kierkegaard: Solving the faith/history problem in *Philosophical Fragments*. *Religious Studies, 51*(4), 455–476.

Corrêa, F. B. (2017). Lima Barreto, elitism, and the emergence of mass society in Brazil (1900s-1920s). *Luso-Brazilian Review, 54*(2), 45–65.

Cruz, A. L. (2013). Paulo Freire's concept of conscientização. In R. Lake & T. Kress (Eds.), *Paulo Freire's intellectual roots: Toward historocity in praxis* (pp. 169–182). London: Bloomsbury.

da Silva, J. R. G. (2014). *Lima Barreto e educação: O protagonismo do oprimido*. Unpublished dissertation. São Paulo: Universidade Nove de Julho.

Darder, A. (2002). *Reinventing Paulo Freire: A pedagogy of love*. Boulder, CO: Westview Press.

Darder, A. (2003). Teaching as an act of love: Reflections on Paulo Freire and his contributions to our lives and our work. In A. Darder, M. Baltondano, & R. D. Torres (Eds.), *The critical pedagogy reader*. London: RoutledgeFalmer.

Darder, A. (2018). *The student guide to Freire's* Pedagogy of the Oppressed. London: Bloomsbury.

Davis, C. (2007). Camus's *La Peste*: Sanitation, rats, and messy ethics. *Modern Language Review, 102*(4), 1008–1020.

Delaune, A. (2020). *Attention and early childhood education*. PhD thesis, University of Canterbury, New Zealand.

Denton, D. E. (1964). Albert Camus: Philosopher of moral concern. *Educational Theory, 14*, 99–127.

Descartes, R. (1911). Discourse on method. In *The philosophical works of Descartes*, vol. 1 (E. S. Haldane & G. R. T. Ross, Trans.). Cambridge: Cambridge University Press.

Dienstag, J. F. (2006). *Pessimism: Philosophy, ethic, spirit*. Princeton, NJ: Princeton University Press.

Earle, S. (2020). The writer for tormented times. *New Statesman*, 29 May – 4 June, 44–47.

Edwards, G. (2019). Language games in the ivory tower: Comparing the *Philosophical Investigations* with Hermann Hesse's *The Glass Bead Game*. *Journal of Philosophy of Education*, *53*(4), 669–687.

Ellsworth, E. (1989). Why doesn't this feel empowering? Working through the repressive myths of critical pedagogy. *Harvard Educational Review*, *59*(3), 297–324.

Eringfeld, S. (2021). Higher education and its post-coronial future: Utopian hopes and dystopian fears at Cambridge University during Covid-19. *Studies in Higher Education*, *46*(1), 146–157.

Escobar, M., Fernandez, A. L., Guevara-Niebla, G. with Freire, P. (1994). *Paulo Freire on higher education: A dialogue at the National University of Mexico*. Albany, NY: State University of New York Press.

Espinoza, O. (2017). Paulo Freire's ideas as an alternative to higher education neoliberal reforms in Latin America. *Journal of Moral Education*, *46*(4), 435–448.

Evans, C. S. (2004). The role of irony in Kierkegaard's *Philosophical Fragments*. *Kierkegaard Studies Yearbook* (pp. 63–79). Berlin: Walter de Gruyter.

Evans, J. E. (2013). *Miguel de Unamuno's quest for faith: A Kierkegaardian understanding of Unamuno's struggle to believe*. Eugene, OR: Pickwick Publications.

Farrell, B. (2018). *Dewey, Freire and student engagement: A critique of tertiary education policy in Ireland and New Zealand*, PhD thesis, University of Canterbury, New Zealand.

Farrell, B., Angel, M. C. N., & Vahl, M. (2017). Hope and utopia in 'post-truth' times: A Freirean approach. *Revista Brasileira de Alfabetização – ABAlf*, *1*(6), 81–97.

Fendt, G. (2019). Reason, feeling, and happiness: Bridging an ancient/modern divide in *The Plague*. *Philosophy and Literature*, *43*(2), 350–368.

Fendt, G. (2020). The Augustinianism of Albert Camus' *The Plague*. *The Heythrop Journal*, *LXI*, 471–482.

Findsen, B. (2007). Freirean philosophy and pedagogy in the adult education context: The case of older adults' learning. *Studies in Philosophy and Education*, *26*, 545–559.

Flecha, R. (2013). Life experiences with Paulo and Nita. *International Journal of Critical Pedagogy*, *5*(1), 17–24.

Flew, T. (2014). Six theories of neoliberalism. *Thesis Eleven*, *122*(1), 49–71.

Foucault, M. (2001). *Madness and civilization*. Abingdon: Routledge.

Fraser, J. W. (1997). Love and history in the work of Paulo Freire. In P. Freire, J. W. Fraser, D. Macedo, T. McKinnon, & W. T. Stokes (Eds.), *Mentoring the mentor: A critical dialogue with Paulo Freire* (pp. 175–199). New York, NY: Peter Lang.

Freire, P. (1972a). *Pedagogy of the oppressed*. Harmondsworth: Penguin.

Freire, P. (1972b). *Cultural action for freedom*. Harmondsworth: Penguin.

Freire, P. (1976). *Education: The practice of freedom*. London: Writers and Readers.

Freire, P. (1978). *Pedagogy in process: The letters to Guinea-Bissau*. London: Writers and Readers.

Freire, P. (1983). The importance of the act of reading. *Journal of Education*, *165*(1), 5–11.

Freire, P. (1985). *The politics of education*. London: MacMillan.

Freire, P. (1987). Letter to North-American teachers. In I. Shor (Ed.), *Freire for the classroom* (pp. 211–214). Portsmouth, NH: Boynton/Cook.

Freire, P. (1993). *Pedagogy of the city*. New York: Continuum.

Freire, P. (1994). *Pedagogy of hope*. New York: Continuum.

Freire, P. (1995). The progressive teacher. In M. de Figueiredo-Cowen & D. Gastadlo (Eds.), *Paulo Freire at the Institute* (pp. 17–24). University of London: Institute of Education.

Freire, P. (1996). *Letters to Cristina: Reflections on my life and work*. London: Routledge.

Freire, P. (1997a). *Pedagogy of the heart*. New York: Continuum.

Freire, P. (1997b). A response. In P. Freire, J. W. Fraser, D. Macedo, T. McKinnon, & W. T. Stokes (Eds.), *Mentoring the mentor: A critical dialogue with Paulo Freire* (pp. 303–329). New York: Peter Lang.

Freire, P. (1998a). *Pedagogy of freedom: Ethics, democracy, and civic courage*. Lanham, Maryland: Rowman and Littlefield.

Freire, P. (1998b). *Teachers as cultural workers: Letters to those who dare teach*. Boulder, CO: Westview Press.

Freire, P. (1998c). *Politics and education*. Los Angeles, CA: UCLA Latin American Center Publications.

Freire, P. (2004). *Pedagogy of indignation*. Boulder, CO: Paradigm Publishers.

Freire, P. (2007). *Daring to dream*. Boulder, CO: Paradigm Publishers.

Freire, P., & Faundez, A. (1989). *Learning to question: A pedagogy of liberation*. Geneva: World Council of Churches.

Freire, P., Fraser, J. W., Macedo, D., McKinnon, T., & Stokes, W. T. (Eds.). (1997). *Mentoring the mentor: A critical dialogue with Paulo Freire*. New York: Peter Lang.

Freire, P., Freire, A. M. A., & de Oliviera, W. F. (2014). *Pedagogy of solidarity*. Walnut Cove, CA: Left Coast Press.

Freire, P., & Macedo, D. (1987). *Literacy: Reading the word and the world*. London: Routledge.

Freire, P., & Macedo, D. (1993). A dialogue with Paulo Freire. In P. McLaren & P. Leonard (Eds.), *Paulo Freire: A critical encounter* (pp. 169–176). London: Routledge.

Freire, P., & Macedo, D. (1995). A dialogue: culture, language, and race. *Harvard Educational Review, 65*(3), 377–402.

Freire, P., & Shor, I. (1987). *A pedagogy for liberation*. London: MacMillan.

Gadotti, M. (2011). Adult education as a human right: The Latin American context and the ecopedagogic perspective. *International Review of Education, 57*, 9–25.

Gadotti, M. (2017). The global impact of Freire's pedagogy. *New Directions for Evaluation, 155*, 17–30.

Gallchóir, C. Ó., & McGarr, O. (2021). An Irish perspective on initial teacher education: How teacher educators can respond to an awareness of the 'absurd'. *Educational Philosophy and Theory*. https://doi.org/10.1080/00131857.2021.1901080.

Gibbons, A. (2012). Difference in the sandpits of the South Pacific: Learning from Albert Camus. *Pacific-Asian Education, 24*(2), 45–55.

Gibbons, A. (2013a). The teaching of tragedy: Narrative and education. *Educational Philosophy and Theory, 45*(11), 1150–1161.

Gibbons, A. (2013b). Tragedy and teaching: The education of narrative. *Educational Philosophy and Theory, 45*(11), 1162–1174.

Gibbs, P. (2015). Happiness and education: Troubling students for their own contentment. *Time and Society, 24*(1), 54–70.

Gibbs, P., & Dean, A. (2014). Troubling the notion of satisfied students. *Higher Education Quarterly, 68*(4), 416–431.

Giroux, H. A. (1983). *Theory and resistance in education: A pedagogy for the opposition.* South Hadley, MA: Bergin & Garvey.

Giroux, H. A. (2010). Rethinking education as the practice of freedom: Paulo Freire and the promise of critical pedagogy. *Truthout*, 1 January 2010.

Glassman, M., & Patton, R. (2014). Capability through participatory democracy: Sen, Freire, and Dewey. *Educational Philosophy and Theory, 46*(12), 1353–1365.

Goodman, P. (1971). *Compulsory miseducation.* Harmondsworth: Penguin.

Gordon, M. (2016). Teachers as absurd heroes: Camus' Sisyphus and the promise of rebellion. *Educational Philosophy and Theory, 48*(6), 589–604.

Götz, I. L. (1987). Camus and the art of teaching. *Educational Theory, 37*(3), 265–276.

Gribble, J. (1983). *Literary education: A revaluation.* Cambridge: Cambridge University Press.

Grugel, J., & Riggirozzi, P. (2012). Post neoliberalism: Rebuilding and reclaiming the state in Latin America. *Development and Change, 43*(1), 1–21.

Guilherme, A., & de Freitas, A. L. S. (2017). "Happiness education": A pedagogical-political commitment. *Policy Futures in Education, 15*(1), 6–19.

Guilherme, A., & Morgan, W. J. (2018). Considering the role of the teacher: Buber, Freire and Gur-Ze'ev. *Educação & Realidade, 43*(3), 783–798.

Hale, G. A. (2002). *Kierkegaard and the ends of language.* Minneapolis, MN: University of Minnesota Press.

Hall, S., Massey, D., & Rustin, M. (2013). After neoliberalism: Analysing the present. *Soundings, 53*, 8–22.

Hannay, A. (1989). Introduction. In S. Kierkegaard, *The sickness unto death* (A. Hannay, Trans.) (pp. 1–32). London: Penguin.

Harrison, V. S. (1997). Kierkegaard's *Philosophical Fragments*: A clarification. *Religious Studies, 33*(4), 455–472.

Harvey, D. (2005). *A brief history of neoliberalism.* Oxford: Oxford University Press.

Hawes, E. (2009). *Camus, a romance.* New York: Grove Press.

Haynes, B. (Ed.). (2009). *Patriotism and citizenship education.* Oxford: Wiley-Blackwell.

Hill, B. V. (1966). Soren Kierkegaard and educational theory. *Educational Theory, 16*(4), 344–353.

Hobson, A. (2017). *Albert Camus and education.* Rotterdam: Sense.

hooks, b. (1993). bell hooks speaking about Paulo Freire – The man, the work. In P. McLaren & P. Leonard (Eds.), *Paulo Freire: A critical encounter* (pp. 146–154). London: Routledge.

Horton, M., & Freire, P. (1990). *We make the road by walking: Conversations on education and social change*. Philadelphia: Temple University Press.

Howland, J. (2006). *Kierkegaard and Socrates: A study in philosophy and faith*. Cambridge: Cambridge University Press.

Illich, I. (1971). *Deschooling society*. Harmondsworth: Penguin.

Jackson, L. (2016). Banking education and the challenges of problem-posing education. In M. A. Peters (Ed.), *Encyclopedia of educational philosophy and theory*. Singapore: Springer.

Jackson, L., & Bingham, C. (2018). Reconsidering happiness in the context of social justice education. *Interchange: A Quarterly Review of Education, 49*, 217–229.

Jackson, S. (2007). Freire re-viewed. *Educational Theory, 57*(2), 199–213.

Jessop, B. (2002). Liberalism, neoliberalism, and urban governance: A state-theoretical perspective. *Antipode*, 452–472.

Jollimore, T., & Barrios, S. (2006). Creating cosmopolitans: The case for literature. *Studies in Philosophy and Education, 25*, 263–283.

Jover Olmeda, G., & Luque, D. (2020). Re-readings of Paulo Freire in the 21st century: Fifty years of *Pedagogy of the Oppressed*, *Educación XX1, 23*(2), 145–164.

Kabel, A., & Phillipson, R. (2021). Structural violence and hope in catastrophic times: From Camus' *The Plague* to Covid-19. *Race & Class, 62*(4), 3–18.

Kee, J. C., & Carr-Chellman, D. J. (2019). Paulo Freire, critical literacy, and Indigenous resistance. *Educational Studies, 55*(1), 89–103.

Kenny, J. (2017). Academic work and performativity. *Higher Education, 74*(5), 897–913.

Kierkegaard, S. (1985). *Philosophical fragments* (H. V. Hong & E. H. Hong, Trans.). Princeton, NJ: Princeton University Press.

Kierkegaard, S. (1987). *Either/or*, 2 vols. (H. V. Hong & E. H. Hong, Trans.). Princeton, NJ: Princeton University Press.

Kierkegaard, S. (1988). *Stages on life's way* (H. V. Hong & E. H. Hong, Trans.). Princeton, NJ: Princeton University Press.

Kierkegaard, S. (1989). *The sickness unto death* (A. Hannay, Trans.). London: Penguin.

Kierkegaard, S. (1998). *Works of love* (H. V. Hong & E. H. Hong, Trans.). Princeton, NJ: Princeton University Press.

Kierkegaard, S. (2009). *Concluding unscientific postscript* (A. Hannay, Trans.). Cambridge: Cambridge University Press.

Kim, T. (2012). *Reasonableness of faith: A study of Kierkegaard's* Philosophical Fragments. New York: Peter Lang.

Kirylo, J. D. (2011). *Paulo Freire: The man from Recife*. New York: Peter Lang.

Kirylo, J. D. (Ed.). (2013). *A critical pedagogy of resistance*. Rotterdam: Sense Publishers.

Kirylo, J. D. (Ed.). (2020). *Reinventing Pedagogy of the Oppressed: Contemporary critical perspectives*. London: Bloomsbury.

Kirylo, J. D., & Boyd, D. (2017). *Paulo Freire: His faith, spirituality, and theology*. Rotterdam: Sense.

Kline, K., & Abowitz, K. K. (2020). Walker Percy's *The Moviegoer*: On the existential novel as educational text. *Educational Theory, 70*(2), 171–185.

Krapp, J. (1999). Time and ethics in Albert Camus's *The Plague*. *University of Toronto Quarterly, 68* (2), 655–676.

Kwak, D.-J. (2001). A new formulation of the ethical self through Kierkegaard's notion of subjectivity: In search of a new moral education. *Asia Pacific Education Review, 2*(1), 3–9.

Lachenal, G., & Thomas, G. (2020). Epidemics have lost the plot. *Bulletin of the History of Medicine, 94*(4), 670–689.

Lake, R., & Kress, T. (2017). Mamma don't put that blue guitar in a museum: Greene and Freire's duet of radical hope in hopeless times. *Review of Education, Pedagogy, and Cultural Studies, 39*(1), 60–75.

Langer, S. K. (1929). The treadmill of systematic doubt. *The Journal of Philosophy, 26*(14), 379–384.

Lankshear, C. (1993). Functional literacy from a Freirean point of view. In P. McLaren & P. Leonard (Eds.), *Paulo Freire: A critical encounter* (pp. 90–118). London: Routledge.

Laverty, M. J. (2014). As luck would have it: Thomas Hardy's *Bildungsroman* on leading a human life. *Studies in Philosophy and Education, 33*(6), 635–646.

Laverty, M. J. (2019). J.M. Coetzee, eros and education. *Journal of Philosophy of Education, 53*(3), 574–588.

Lewis, T. (2011). The future of the image in critical pedagogy. *Studies in Philosophy and Education, 30*(1), 37–51.

Lewkowicz, J. (2015). Post-neoliberalism: Lessons from South America. *openDemocracyUK*, 9 February.

Liu, K. (2014). *Conscientization and the cultivation of conscience*. New York: Peter Lang.

Lund, G. (2011). A plague of silence: Social hygiene and the purification of the nation in Camus's La Peste. *Symposium: A Quarterly Journal in Modern Literatures, 65*(2), 134–157.

Macedo, D. (1997). An anti-method pedagogy: A Freirian perspective. In P. Freire, J. W. Fraser, D. Macedo, T. McKinnon, & W. T. Stokes (Eds.), *Mentoring the mentor: A critical dialogue with Paulo Freire* (pp. 1–9). New York: Peter Lang.

Macedo, D. (2013). Situating pedagogy of the oppressed after Nita Freire. *International Journal of Critical Pedagogy, 5*(1), 82–100.

Mackie, R. (1980). Contributions to the thought of Paulo Freire. In R. Mackie (Ed.), *Literacy and revolution: The pedagogy of Paulo Freire* (pp. 93–119). London: Pluto Press.

Madero, C. (2015). Theological dynamics of Paulo Freire's educational theory: An essay to assist the work of Catholic educators. *International Studies in Catholic Education, 7*(2), 122–133.

Malesic, J. (2007). Illusion and offense in *Philosophical Fragments*: Kierkegaard's inversion of Feuerbach's critique of Christianity. *International Journal for Philosophy of Religion, 62*(1), 43–55.

Margonis, F. (2003). Paulo Freire and post-colonial dilemmas. *Studies in Philosophy and Education, 22*(2), 145–156.

Marshall, J. D. (2008). Philosophy as literature. *Educational Philosophy and Theory, 40*(3), 383–393.

Mayo, P. (1997). Tribute to Paulo Freire (1921–1997). *International Journal of Lifelong Education, 16*(5), 365–370.

Mayo, P. (1999). *Gramsci, Freire and adult education: Possibilities for transformative action.* London: Zed Books.

Mayo, P. (2004). *Liberating praxis: Paulo Freire's legacy for radical education and politics.* New York: Praeger.

Mayo, P. (2013). *Echoes from Freire for a critically engaged pedagogy.* New York: Bloomsbury.

McCreary, M. L. (2011). Deceptive love: Kierkegaard on mystification and deceiving into the truth. *The Journal of Religious Ethics, 39*(1), 25–47.

McKeown, M., Edgar, F., Spandler, H., & Carey, L. (2018). Conscientization and transformation in the workplace: New forms of democracy for mental health services. In A. Melling & R. Pilkington (Eds.), *Paulo Freire and Transformative Education* (pp. 153–163). London: Palgrave Macmillan.

McKnight, D. (2004). Kierkegaard and the despair of the aesthetic existence in teaching. *Journal of Curriculum Theorizing, 20*(1), 59–80.

McLaren, P. (1999). A pedagogy of possibility: Reflecting upon Paulo Freire's politics of education. *Educational Researcher, 28,* 49–56.

McLaren, P. (2000). *Che Guevara, Paulo Freire, and the pedagogy of revolution.* Lanham, MD: Rowman and Littlefield.

McMenamin, T. (2017). Lessons from life and love in Murdoch's work. In M. A. Peters (Ed.), *Encyclopedia of Educational Philosophy and Theory* (pp. 1–5). Singapore: Springer.

McPherson, I. (2001). Kierkegaard as an educational thinker: Communication through and across ways of being. *Journal of Philosophy of Education, 35*(2), 157–174.

Mercer, D. E. (2001). *Kierkegaard's living room: The relation between faith and history in Philosophical Fragments.* Montreal and Kingston: McGill-Queen's University Press.

Ministry of Education. (2002). *Tertiary education strategy, 2002–07.* Wellington: Ministry of Education (Office of the Associate Minister of Education – Tertiary Education).

Ministry of Education. (2006). *Tertiary education strategy, 2007–12.* Wellington: Ministry of Education (Office of the Associate Minister of Education – Tertiary Education).

Ministry of Education. (2009). *Tertiary education strategy, 2010–15.* Wellington: Ministry of Education (Office of the Minister for Tertiary Education).

Ministry of Education. (2020). *The Statement of National Education and Learning Priorities (NELP) and Tertiary Education Strategy (TES).* Wellington: Ministry of Education.

Misiaszek, G. W. (2018). A critical scholar's journey in China: A brief Freirean analysis of insider–outsider tensions. *Educational Philosophy and Theory, 50*(12), 1133–1143.

Morrow, R. A., & Torres, C. A. (2002). *Reading Freire and Habermas: Critical pedagogy and transformative social change.* New York: Teachers College Press.

Murdoch, I. (2001). *The sovereignty of good.* London and New York: Routledge.

Murillo, F. (2021). The curriculum of the plague. *Prospects.* https://doi.org/10.1007/s11125-020-09535-5

Murrell, P. C. (1997). Digging again the family wells: A Freirian literacy framework as emancipatory pedagogy for African-American children. In P. Freire, J. W. Fraser, D. Macedo, T. McKinnon, & W. T. Stokes (Eds.), *Mentoring the mentor: A critical dialogue with Paulo Freire* (pp. 19–58). New York: Peter Lang.

Nelson, D. (2008). A new Glass Bead Game: Redesigning the academy. *Paideusis, 17*(2), 39–49.

Neumann, J. W. (2011). Critical pedagogy and faith. *Educational Theory, 61*(5), 601–619.

New Zealand Government. (2014). *Tertiary education strategy, 2014–2019*. Wellington: Ministry of Education and Ministry of Business, Innovation and Employment.

New Zealand Productivity Commission. (2016). New models of tertiary education: Issues paper. www.productivity.govt.nz/inquirycontent/tertiary-education

New Zealand Productivity Commission. (2017a). *New models of tertiary education: Final Report.* www.productivity.govt.nz/inquiry-content/tertiary-education

New Zealand Productivity Commission. (2017b). New models of tertiary education are coming, ready or not. Press release, 21 March 2017.

Nieto Ángel, M. C., Maciel, V. M., & Farrell, B. (2020). Critical pedagogy, dialogue and tolerance: A learning to disagree framework. In S. L. Macrine (Ed.), *Critical pedagogy in uncertain times: Hope and possibilities* (139–158). London: Palgrave Macmillan.

Noddings, N. (1991). *Women and evil*. Berkeley, CA: University of California Press.

Novacevski, M. (2021). Pestilence in planning: Why Camus is a beacon for our times. *Planning Theory & Practice, 22*(2), 329–335.

Nowachek, M. T. (2014). Living within the sacred tension: Kierkegaard's Climacean works as a guide for Christian existence. *The Heythrop Journal, 55*(5), 883–902.

O'Cadiz, M. D. P., Wong, L., & Torres, C. A. (1998). *Education and democracy: Paulo Freire, social movements and educational reform in Sao Paulo*. Boulder, CO: Westview Press.

Oliver, T. (1973). Camus, man, and education. *Educational Theory, 23*(3), 224–229.

Palmer, F. (1992). *Literature and moral understanding: A philosophical essay on ethics, aesthetics, education, and culture*. Oxford: Clarendon Press.

Pashby, K. (2011). Cultivating global citizens: Planting new seeds or pruning the perennials? Looking for the citizen-subject in global citizenship education theory. *Globalisation, Societies and Education, 9*(3–4), 427–442.

PBRF Review Panel. (2020). *E koekoe te tūī, e ketekete te kākā, e kūkū te kererū: Toward the Tertiary Research Excellence Evaluation (TREE)*. The Report of the PBRF Review Panel. Wellington: Ministry of Education.

Peters, M. (1999). Freire and postmodernism. In P. Roberts (Ed.), *Paulo Freire, politics and pedagogy: Reflections from Aotearoa-New Zealand* (pp. 113–122). Palmerston North: Dunmore Press.

Peters, M. A. (2020). *The Plague*: Human resilience and the collective response to catastrophe. *Educational Philosophy and Theory* (early online version). https://doi.org/10.1080/00131857.2020.1745921

Peters, M. A., & Besley, T. (Eds.). (2015). *Paulo Freire: The global legacy*. New York: Peter Lang.

Peters, M. A., Britton, A., & Blee, H. (Eds.). (2008). *Global citizenship education: Philosophy, theory and pedagogy*. Rotterdam: Sense Publishers.

Peters, M. A., & Roberts, P. (2011). *The virtues of openness*. Boulder, CO: Paradigm Publishers.

Petrovic, J. E., & Kuntz, A. M. (Eds.). (2014). *Citizenship education around the world: Local contexts and global possibilities*. New York: Routledge.

Petrovic, J. E., & Rolstad, K. (2016). Educating for autonomy: Reading Rousseau and Freire toward a philosophy of unschooling. *Policy Futures in Education, 14*, 1–17.

Phillips, J. (2020). "There is no sun without the shadow and it is essential to know the night": Albert Camus' philosophy of the absurd and Shaun Tan's *The Red Tree*. *Children's Literature in Education, 51*, 5–20.

Pillen, H., McNaughton, D., & Ward, P. R. (2020). Critical consciousness development: A systematic review of empirical studies. *Health Promotion International, 35*(6), 1519–1530.

Pinar, W. F. (2006a). *The synoptic text today and other essays: Curriculum development after the reconceptualization*. New York: Peter Lang.

Pinar, W. F. (2006b). Literary study as educational research. In K. Tobin & J. Kincheloe (Eds.), *Doing educational research* (pp. 347–377). Rotterdam: Sense Publishers.

Pinar, W. F. (2011). *The character of curriculum studies: Bildung, currere, and the recurring question of the subject*. New York: Palgrave Macmillan.

Pinar, W. F. (2014). Curriculum research in the United States. In W. F. Pinar (Ed.), *International handbook of curriculum research* (2nd edn, pp. 521–532). New York: Routledge.

Pinar, W. F. (2015). *Educational experience as lived: Knowledge, history, alterity – The selected writings of William F. Pinar*. New York: Routledge.

Postman, N., & Weingartner, D. (1971). *Teaching as a subversive activity*. Harmondsworth: Penguin.

Principe, J. D. (2020). The decency of Albert Camus. *Renascence, 72*(2), 99–120.

Reigota, M. (2013). Affection, environmental education and politics: Encounters with Nita and Paulo Freire. *International Journal of Critical Pedagogy, 5*(1), 41–49.

Reveley, J. (2015). School-based mindfulness training and the economisation of attention: A Stieglerian view. *Educational Philosophy and Theory, 47*(8), 804–821.

Reveley, J. (2018). Embracing the humanistic vision: Recurrent themes in Peter Roberts' recent writings. *Educational Philosophy and Theory, 50*(3), 312–321.

Roberts, P. (1997). A critique of the NZQA policy reforms. In M. Olssen & K. Morris Matthews (Eds.), *Education Policy in New Zealand: The 1990s and Beyond* (pp. 162–189). Palmerston North: Dunmore Press.

Roberts, P. (1999a). A dilemma for critical educators? *Journal of Moral Education, 28*(1), 19–30.

Roberts, P. (Ed.). (1999b). *Paulo Freire, politics and pedagogy: Reflections from Aotearoa-New Zealand*. Palmerston North: Dunmore Press.

Roberts, P. (2000). *Education, literacy, and humanization: Exploring the work of Paulo Freire*. Westport, CT: Bergin and Garvey.

Roberts, P. (2004). Neoliberalism, knowledge and inclusiveness. *Policy Futures in Education, 2*(2), 350–364.

Roberts, P. (2006). Performativity, measurement and research: A critique of performance-based research funding in New Zealand. In J. Ozga, T. Popkewitz, & T. Seddon (Eds.), *World yearbook of education 2006: Education research and policy* (pp. 185–199). London: Routledge.

Roberts, P. (2007a). Neoliberalism, performativity and research. *International Review of Education, 53*(4), 349–365.

Roberts, P. (2007b). Intellectuals, tertiary education and questions of difference. *Educational Philosophy and Theory, 39*(5), 480–493.

Roberts, P. (2008a). Teaching, learning and ethical dilemmas: Lessons from Albert Camus. *Cambridge Journal of Education, 38*(4), 529–542.

Roberts, P. (2008b). Bridging literary and philosophical genres: Judgement, reflection and education in Camus' The Fall. *Educational Philosophy and Theory, 40*(7), 873–887.

Roberts, P. (2010). *Paulo Freire in the 21st century: Education, dialogue and transformation*. Boulder, CO, and London, UK: Paradigm Publishers.

Roberts, P. (2012). *From West to East and back again: An educational reading of Hermann Hesse's later work*. Rotterdam: Sense Publishers.

Roberts, P. (2013). Academic dystopia: Knowledge, performativity and tertiary education. *The Review of Education, Pedagogy, and Cultural Studies, 35*(1), 27–43.

Roberts, P. (2014). Tertiary education and critical citizenship. In J. E. Petrovic & A. M. Kuntz (Eds.), *Citizenship education around the world: Local contexts and global possibilities* (pp. 220–236). New York: Routledge.

Roberts, P. (Ed.). (2015). *Shifting focus: Strangers and strangeness in literature and education*. New York: Routledge.

Roberts, P. (2016). *Happiness, hope, and despair: Rethinking the role of education*. New York: Peter Lang.

Roberts, P., & Freeman-Moir, J. (2013). *Better worlds: Education, art, and utopia*. Lanham, MD: Lexington Books.

Roberts, P., Gibbons, A., & Heraud, R. (2015). *Education, ethics and existence: Camus and the human condition*. New York: Routledge.

Roberts, P., & Saeverot, H. (2018). *Education and the limits of reason: Reading Dostoevsky, Tolstoy and Nabokov*. New York: Routledge.

Rocha, S. D. (2019). "Ser mais": The personalism of Paulo Freire. In M. Laverty (Ed.), *Philosophy of education 2018* (pp. 371–384). Urbana, IL: Philosophy of Education Society.

Rosenthal, J. (2020). In self-isolation with The Plague. *The Hedgehog Review*, Summer, 9–11.

Rossatto, C. (2005). *Engaging Paulo Freire's pedagogy of possibility: From blind to transformative optimism*. Lanham, MD: Rowman and Littlefield.

Rozas Gomez, C. (2007). The possibility of justice: The work of Paulo Freire and difference. *Studies in Philosophy and Education, 26*, 561–570.

Rozas Gomez, C. (2013). Strangers and orphans: Knowledge and mutuality in Mary Shelley's Frankenstein. *Educational Philosophy and Theory, 45*(4), 360–370.

Rule, P. (2011). Bakhtin and Freire: Dialogue, dialectic and boundary learning. *Educational Philosophy and Theory, 43*(9), 924–942.

Saeverot, H. (2011). Kierkegaard, seduction, and existential education. *Studies in Philosophy and Education, 30*(6), 557–572.

Saeverot, H. (2013). Irony, deception and subjective truth: Principles for existential teaching. *Studies in Philosophy and Education, 32*, 503–513.

Saevi, T. (2011). Lived relationality as fulcrum for pedagogical-ethical practice. *Studies in Philosophy and Education, 30*(5), 455–461.

Saito, E. (2021). Educational polyphony for a contemplative under tragic tension: Implications from the early life of Smerdyakov in *The Brothers Karamazov*. *Journal of Beliefs & Values*, 1–11. https://doi.org/10.1080/13617672.2021.1982559.

Salcedo, F. X. R. (2020). Albert Camus' *La Peste* and the Covid-19 pandemic: Exile and imprisonment, suffering and death, defiance and heroism. *Journal for the Study of Religions and Ideologies, 19*(56), 136–149.

Santos, F. D. (2017). *Education and the boarding school novel: The work of José Régio*. Rotterdam: Sense.

Sartwell, C. (1991). Doubt and faith: Santayana and Kierkegaard on fundamental belief. *Transactions of the Charles S. Peirce Society, 27*(2), 179–195.

Schugurensky, D. (2011). *Paulo Freire*. London: Continuum.

Schwarcz, L. M. (2014). Introduction. In L. Barreto (Ed.), *The sad end of Policarpo Quaresma* (M. Carlyon, Trans.). London: Penguin.

Schwarcz, L. M. (2017). Sad visionary: Lima Barreto and racial inequality in Brazil. Video retrieved from the Library of Congress. https://www.loc.gov/item/webcast-8245/.

Schwieler, E. (2017). Faulkner, literature, and learning. In M. Peters (Ed.), *Encyclopedia of educational philosophy and theory*. Singapore: Springer. https://doi.org/10.1007/978-981-287-532-7_555-1

Serra, M. V. (2011). Time, the city and Lima Barreto. In L. Barreto (Ed.), *Triste fim de Policarpo Quaresma/The sad end of Policarpo Quaresma* (M. Carlyon, Trans.) (pp. 28–41). Rio de Janeiro: Instituto Cultural Cidade Viva.

Sharpe, M. (2016a). Socratic ironies: Reading Hadot, reading Kierkegaard. *Sophia, 55*, 409–435.

Sharpe, M. (2016b). The plague and the Panopticon: Camus, with and against the total critiques of modernity. *Thesis Eleven, 133*(1), 59–79.

Sherman, A. L. (1980). Two views of emotion in the writings of Paulo Freire. *Educational Theory, 30*(1), 35–38.

Shim, S. H. (2007). A philosophical investigation of the role of teachers: A synthesis of Plato, Confucius, Buber, and Freire. *Teaching and Teacher Education, 24*, 515–535.

Shor, I. (1980). *Critical teaching and everyday life*. Boston, MA: South End Press.

Shor, I. (Ed.). (1987). *Freire for the classroom*. Portsmouth, NH: Boynton/Cook.

Shor, I. (1993). Education is politics: Paulo Freire's critical pedagogy. In P. McLaren & P. Leonard (Eds.), *Paulo Freire: A Critical Encounter* (pp. 25–35). London: Routledge.

Shyman, E. (2011). A comparison of the concepts of democracy and experience in a sample of major works by Dewey and Freire. *Educational Philosophy and Theory, 43*(10), 1035–1046.

Sichel, B. A. (1992). Education and thought in Virginia Woolf's *To the Lighthouse*. *Philosophy of Education 1992*. Urbana-Champaign, IL: Philosophy of Education Society.

Siegel, H. (1997). Teaching, reasoning, and Dostoevsky's *The brothers Karamazov*. In H. Siegel (Ed.), *Rationality Redeemed? Further dialogues on an educational ideal* (pp. 39–54). New York and London: Routledge.

Smith, G. (1999). Paulo Freire: Lessons in transformative praxis. In P. Roberts (Ed.), *Paulo Freire, politics and pedagogy: Reflections from Aotearoa-New Zealand*. Dunmore Press: Palmerston North.

Snauwaert, D. (2011). Social justice and the philosophical foundations of critical peace education: Exploring Nussbaum, Sen, and Freire. *Journal of Peace Education, 8*(3), 315–331.

Springer, S. (2015). Postneoliberalism? *Review of Radical Political Economics, 47*(1), 5–17.

Stelson, E. (2021). COVID and Camus: Reflections on *The Plague*, collective experience, and qualitative inquiry during a pandemic. *Qualitative Social Work, 20*(1–2), 41–47.

Suissa, J. (2017). Pedagogies of indignation and *The lives of others*. *Policy Futures in Education, 15*(7–8), 874–890.

Tan, C. (2018a). Wither teacher-directed learning? Freirean and Confucian insights. *The Educational Forum, 82*(4), 461–474.

Tan, C. (2018b). To be more fully human: Freire and Confucius. *Oxford Review of Education, 44*(4), 370–382.

Taylor, P. V. (1993). *The texts of Paulo Freire*. Buckingham: Open University Press.

Thornton, S. (2019). The educational cost of philosophical suicide: What it means to be lucid. *Educational Philosophy and Theory, 51*(6), 608–618.

Tiainen, K., Leiviskä, A., & Brunila, K. (2019). Democratic education for hope: Contesting the neoliberal common sense. *Studies in Philosophy and Education, 38*, 641–655.

Todd, O. (2000). *Albert Camus: A life* (B. Ivry, Trans.). New York: Carroll & Graf.

Todd, S. (2018). Culturally reimagining education: Publicity, aesthetics and socially engaged art practice. *Educational Philosophy and Theory, 50*(10), 970–980.

Toh, G. (2017). Provocative encounters reflecting struggles with change: Power and coercion in a Japanese university situation. *Policy Futures in Education, 15*(4), 512–525.

Toh, G. (2018). Anatomizing and extrapolating 'Do not publish' as oppression, silencing, and denial. *Critical Inquiry in Language Studies, 15*(4), 258–281.

Torres, C. A. (1994a). Education and the archeology of consciousness: Freire and Hegel. *Educational Theory, 44*(4), 429–445.

Torres, C. A. (1994b). Introduction – Intellectuals and university life: Paulo Freire and higher education. In M. Escobar, A. L. Fernandez, & G. Guevara-Niebla, with P. Freire (Eds.), *Paulo Freire on higher education: A dialogue at the National University of Mexico* (pp. 1–25). Albany, NY: State University of New York Press.

Torres, C. A. (1998). Introduction: The political pedagogy of Paulo Freire. In P. Freire (Ed.), *Politics and education* (pp. 1–15). Los Angeles, CA: UCLA Latin American Center Publications.

Torres, C. A. (2009). *Education and neoliberal globalization*. New York: Routledge.

Torres, C. A. (2014). *First Freire: Early writings in social justice education*. New York: Teachers College Press.

Torres, C. A. (Ed.). (2019). *The Wiley handbook of Paulo Freire*. Oxford: Wiley-Blackwell.

Tubbs, N. (2005). Kierkegaard. *Journal of Philosophy of Education, 39*(2), 387–409.

Tuffuor, A. N., & Payne, R. (2017). Isolation and suffering related to serious and terminal illness: Metaphors and lessons from Albert Camus' novel, *The Plague. Journal of Pain and Symptom Management, 54*(3), 400–403.

Unamuno, M. de (1972). *The tragic sense of life in men and nations* (A. Kerrigan, Trans.). Princeton, NJ: Princeton University Press.

Unuajohwofia, H. O., & Orhero, M. I. (2021). Epidemics, lockdowns, and hypocrisy: The case of simulated reality. *Social Sciences and Humanities Open, 4*, 100169, 1–7.

Vahl, M. (2018). *A pedagogy of oppression: The politics of literacy in Brazil, 1971–1989*. PhD thesis, University of Canterbury, New Zealand.

Vahl, M. M., Arriada, E., & Nogueira, G. M. (2021). Autoritarismo e esperança: Costurando fios entre Paulo Freire e José Cardoso Piresmônica ('Authoritarianism and hope: Sewing threads between Paulo Freire and José Cardoso Pires'). *Revista Práxis Educacional, 17*(47), 1–20.

Valente, L. F. (2013). From synthesis to difference: Lima Barreto's parodic ufanismo. In L. Aidoo & D. F. Silva (Eds.), *Lima Barreto: New critical perspectives* (pp. 153–165). Lanham, MD: Lexington Books.

Vandekerckhove, W. (2020). COVID, existentialism and crisis philosophy. *Philosophy of Management, 19*, 127–132.

Veugelers, W. (2011). The moral and the political in global citizenship: Appreciating differences in education. *Globalisation, Societies and Education, 9*(3–4), 473–485.

Veugelers, W. (2017). The moral in Paulo Freire's educational work: What moral education can learn from Paulo Freire. *Journal of Moral Education, 46*(4), 412–421.

Vlieghe, J. (2018). Rethinking emancipation with Freire and Rancière: A plea for a thing-centred pedagogy. *Educational Philosophy and Theory, 50*(10), 917–927.

Walker, J. (1980). The end of dialogue: Paulo Freire on politics and education. In R. Mackie (Ed.), *Literacy and revolution: The pedagogy of Paulo Freire* (pp. 120–150). London: Pluto Press.

Walker, J. (2008). Conspirators in a neo-liberal agenda? Adult educators in second-chance Private Training Establishments. *Journal of Adult & Continuing Education, 14*(1), 55–73.

Walker, J. (2009). Towards alternative lifelong learning(s): What Freire can still teach us. *Rizoma Freireano, 3*, 1–11.

Walker, J. (2020). Comparing adult education systems: Canada and Aotearoa New Zealand. *Zeitschrift für Weiterbildungsforschung, 43*, 241–257.

Wasserman, R. R. N. (1992). Lima Barreto, the text and the margin: On *Policarpo Quaresma*. *Modern Language Studies, 22*(3), 53–69.

Wasserman, R. R. N. (2008). Race, nation, representation: Machado de Assis and Lima Barreto. *Luso-Brazilian Review, 45*(2), 84–106.

Webster, S. (2009). *Educating for meaningful lives through existential spirituality*. Rotterdam: Sense Publishers.

Webster, S. (2016). The existential individual *alone* within Freire's socio-political solidarity. In M. A. Peters (Ed.), *Encyclopedia of educational philosophy and theory*. Singapore: Springer.

Weddington, H. S. (2007). The education of Sisyphus: Absurdity, educative transformation, and suicide. *Journal of Transformative Education, 5*(2), 119–133.

Weil, S. (1997). *Gravity and grace* (A. Wills, Trans.). Lincoln: Bison Books.

Weil, S. (2001). *Waiting for God* (E. Craufurd, Trans.). New York: Perennial Classics.

Weiler, K. (1991). Paulo Freire and a feminist pedagogy of difference. *Harvard Educational Review, 61*(4), 449–474.

Weiner, E. J. (2003). Secretary Paulo Freire and the democratization of power: Toward a theory of transformative leadership. *Educational Philosophy and Theory, 35*(1), 89–106.

Wilcock, N. (2020). The incoherence of the interactional and the institutional within Freire's politico-educational project. *Studies in Philosophy and Education, 39*(4), 399–414.

Williams, E. (2020). Editorial. *Journal of Philosophy of Education, 54*(3), 489–491.

Williams, G. W. (2012). Irony as the birth of Kierkegaard's "single individual" and the beginning of politics. *Toronto Journal of Theology, 28*(2), 309–318.

Wivestad, S. M. (2011). Conditions for "upbuilding": A reply to Nigel Tubbs' reading of Kierkegaard. *Journal of Philosophy of Education, 45*(4), 613–625.

Zaretsky, R. (2010). *Albert Camus: Elements of a life*. Ithaca, NY: Cornell University Press.

Zaretsky, R. (2020a). Out of a clear blue sky: Camus's *The Plague* and coronavirus. *Times Literary Supplement*, 10 April 2020.

Zaretsky, R. (2020b). The unwilling guide: Camus's *The Plague*. *Social Research, 87*(2), 297–298.

Zembylas, M. (2020). (Un)happiness and social justice education: Ethical, political and pedagogic lessons. *Ethics and Education, 15*(1), 18–32.

Zook, D. C. (2008). The irony of it all: Søren Kierkegaard and the anxious pleasures of civil society. *British Journal for the History of Philosophy, 16*(2), 393–419.

Credits

The author and publisher gratefully acknowledge permission to reproduce material from the following sources.

An earlier version of Chapter One was published as Roberts, P. (2017). Paulo Freire. In G. W. Noblit (Ed.), *Oxford research encyclopedia of education* (pp. 1–24). Oxford: Oxford University Press. https://doi.org/10.1093/acrefore/9780190264093.013.10. With the permission of Oxford University Press (oxfordre.com/education).

Chapter Two is based on Roberts, P. (2017). Learning to live with doubt: Kierkegaard, Freire, and critical pedagogy. *Policy Futures in Education*, 15(7/8), 834–848. Copyright © 2017 Sage Publications. https://doi.org/10.1177/1478210317736225. This material is included under Sage's gratis re-use policy for authors.

Chapter Three is an updated version of Roberts, P. (2017). Impure neoliberalism: A Freirean critique of dominant trends in higher education. *Rizoma Freireano*, 22, 1–18 (http://www.rizoma-freireano.org/). With the permission of the Instituto Paulo Freire de España (www.institutpaulofreire.org).

Chapter Four first appeared, in substantially similar form, as Roberts, P. (2019). Thesis supervision: A Freirean approach. In C. A. Torres (Ed.), *The Wiley handbook of Paulo Freire* (pp. 521–534). Oxford: Wiley-Blackwell. With the permission of the Executive Editor, Wiley.

Material in Chapter Five is reprinted by permission from Springer Nature: *Studies in Philosophy and Education*, 'Epistemology, ethics and education: Addressing dilemmas of difference in the work of Paulo Freire', *22*(2), 157–173, Peter Roberts, Copyright © 2003 Springer Nature.

Chapter Seven is based on Roberts, P. (2021). Conscientization, compassion and madness: Freire, Barreto, and the limits of education. *Review of Education, Pedagogy and Cultural Studies*, *43*, 1–21. https://doi.org/10.1080/10714413.2021.1890510. Reprinted by permission of Informa UK Limited, trading as Taylor & Francis Group, www.tandfonline.com.

OMPLICATED

A BOOK SERIES OF CURRICULUM STUDIES

Reframing the curricular challenge educators face after a decade of school deform, the books published in Peter Lang's Complicated Conversation Series testify to the ethical demands of our time, our place, our profession. What does it mean for us to teach now, in an era structured by political polarization, economic destabilization, and the prospect of climate catastrophe? Each of the books in the Complicated Conversation Series provides provocative paths, theoretical and practical, to a very different future. In this resounding series of scholarly and pedagogical interventions into the nightmare that is the present, we hear once again the sound of silence breaking, supporting us to rearticulate our pedagogical convictions in this time of terrorism, reframing curriculum as committed to the complicated conversation that is intercultural communication, self-understanding, and global justice.

The series editor is

> Dr. William F. Pinar
> Department of Curriculum Studies
> 2125 Main Mall
> Faculty of Education
> University of British Columbia
> Vancouver, British Columbia V6T 1Z4
> CANADA

To order other books in this series, please contact our Customer Service Department:

> peterlang@presswarehouse.com (within the U.S.)
> orders@peterlang.com (outside the U.S.)

Or browse online by series:

> www.peterlang.com

www.ingramcontent.com/pod-product-compliance
Lightning Source LLC
Chambersburg PA
CBHW061717300426
44115CB00014B/2732